COOKING
FOR CASH

JENNIFER CURRY

DAVID & CHARLES
Newton Abbot   London   North Pomfret (Vt)

To my former business partner, Ina, with thanks and affection

British Library Cataloguing in Publication Data

Curry, Jennifer
  Cooking for cash.
  1. Caterers and catering
  I. Title
  647'.95'0941   TX943

  ISBN 0 7153 8423 6

Photoset by Typesetters (Birmingham) Ltd,
and printed in Great Britain
by Billings Ltd, Worcester,
for David & Charles (Publishers) Limited
Brunel House Newton Abbot Devon

Published in the United States of America
by David & Charles Inc
North Pomfret Vermont 05053 USA

Contents

Acknowledgements

Of the many people who helped me with the compilation of this book, my special thanks must go to all the cooks I spoke to, not only those whose interviews are reproduced here, but also those who generously gave up their valuable time to talk to me about their pleasures and problems *without* getting into print. I am also immensely grateful to the army of friends and acquaintances who introduced me to freelance cooks and catering ventures throughout the country.

Without these two groups of people – the caterers and their clients – *Cooking for Cash* could never have been written.

Introduction

Cooking for cash is at present a growth industry, several factors having combined to make it an increasingly popular activity. The current high level of unemployment means that many people, particularly women, who would normally be part of the country's workforce, find themselves without regular work and are consequently suffering the double irritant of not having enough to do to satisfy their energies and potential creativity, and of not having sufficient funds to maintain the standard of living they have come to expect. The government is aware of the damage done to individuals who want to work but cannot find employment and is prepared, in some cases, to offer help in the form of training courses so that those who wish to develop a new or latent skill will be better equipped to help themselves.

Home-based catering, which can take many forms depending upon a cook's interests, skills, amenities, time available and place in which he or she lives, is a very flexible job. It can be fitted in with many other commitments, including the care of a young family or older relatives, a busy social life or other activities and concerns. The variety of opportunity available means that each individual cook can fashion and dovetail the work to fit in with his or her particular interests, temperament and way of doing things.

The fact that in many families both partners go out to work full-time, and often earn a generous salary between them, means that there is constant demand for home-based cooks to help with their entertaining and social functions, or even the day-to-day business of keeping their fridge and freezer filled. There is also at the moment – and it shows no sign of being a passing phase – a groundswell of reaction against synthetic, tinned, frozen, convenience or manufactured foods, so that not only party-givers, but also shops, health food stores, delicatessens, pubs, small restaurants and cafés are anxious to buy homemade dishes cooked from wholesome fresh materials, knowing full well that they will be assured of regular and enthusiastic customers. As people become more prosperous – and it is a strange fact that despite high unemployment large numbers of people in this country *are* enjoying an affluent standard of living – they want more individuality and high-quality personal service.

Taking all this into account, it becomes clear that the time is ripe for someone who likes the idea of making money by cooking to turn the dream into a reality. Thousands of people are doing it already, very successfully, but there is room for many more. However, if the reality is going to be a satisfying and profitable new career, securely based on a well-organised and viable business, it should not be rushed into too eagerly. There is a lot of groundwork to be covered first of all, and if this is not done thoroughly the venture could end in disaster, leaving behind it the double damage of money down the drain and a dented ego.

This book will endeavour to lead you step by step from the first glimmering of the idea to the actual venture into professional catering, so that you can be guaranteed success on a plate. If you have already taken the first steps, it may be able to give you one or two tips about improving your organisation and profitability or extending your range and versatility. And to give you confidence, and the feeling that you are not alone in a new and unknown world, there are personal accounts of their own efforts and struggles, methods and mistakes, but mainly satisfactions, from just a few of the large army of freelance cooks who are already running worth-while catering projects, either for pocket money or substantial profit, but always with pleasure.

1
Check Your Skills

The successful self-employed cook needs a certain amount of basic practical equipment, which will be dealt with in detail in chapter 4, but the most important items of equipment are your **hands** and your **head**. In other words, you need practical skill and creative imagination, the right temperament and organisational ability.

Before you decide whether this really is the job for you and how it can be tailored to your own needs, you should ask yourself some searching questions and attempt to come up with some honest answers. First, and by far the most important:

- do I positively enjoy cooking?

Only if you can answer a resounding 'yes' to that one are you ready to tackle the other questions on the list.

Practical Skills and Creative Imagination

- am I a good and versatile cook with a large variety of dishes at my fingertips? Alternatively, have I the time, will and ability to increase the range of my menus to professional standards, perhaps by doing extra training?
- can I cook happily for large numbers or only for small groups?
- can I make food look good as well as taste good, and am I prepared to take pains with presentation?

Temperament

- have I sufficient self-discipline and determination to cook when I'm not really feeling in the right mood?

- am I thoroughly reliable and know that I will always come up with the goods, despite any personal problems or difficulties that might arise?
- have I the energy, stamina and physical strength and health to work long hours, perhaps under stress, when the bookings are flooding in?
- have I sufficient self-confidence and personal resources not to become worried and demoralised when the bookings aren't even trickling in?
- can I cope with the insecurity which is an essential ingredient of self-employment?
- can I mix comfortably and easily with people from all walks of life? Can I cope with customers who might treat me as a servant or menial, instead of a skilled professional?
- am I able to make decisions and stand by them?
- am I tough enough, but also diplomatic enough, to do things which are necessary though not very pleasant (for example, standing up to an unreasonable customer who is not keeping to his part of the bargain; insisting on prompt payment; pointing out mistakes or inadequacies to an assistant or partner who is not doing his or her job properly; complaining to suppliers who are not providing materials of sufficient quality or who are not keeping to the delivery time or prices agreed)?
- can I go it alone and work entirely on my own? (The one sentence I heard again and again from the cooks I interviewed was: 'The kitchen is a very lonely place'. Cooking, like many other freelance activities, is for the most part a very solitary job. If you are not happy in your own company, you must work out carefully beforehand how much solitude catering will impose upon you, and how much you can survive.)
- do I prefer to be part of a group? And if I am part of a group, can I work as one of a team of equals or do I prefer either to give the orders or have someone else take the responsibility and make the decisions on my behalf?

Organisational Ability

- am I a good organiser? Can I keep calm in a crisis and cope with it?

- have I a good business head? Am I able to market, budget and charge sensibly? If not, can I learn?
- have I enough savings to provide the initial financial layout required? Or am I likely to be able to raise a loan to get my business launched?
- do I need to earn a reasonable living from my cooking which will be my primary source of income? Or am I simply interested in adding to an existing income by exploiting a profitable hobby?

By the time you have considered all these questions and your answers to them, you should know whether you really want to cook for cash, whether you already have what it takes to do so or whether you need to brush up your skills before you get going. Fortunately, there are several ways of improving your culinary versatility, your business ability and your organisational powers. Some of them will cost you money, some of them are free and some of them might even pay you while you retrain.

First of all, you should pay a visit to the largest library in your neighbourhood and become familiar with the relevant books on its shelves and the other services it has to offer. If you haven't yet got to grips with its indexing system, now is the time to start as it will have books you might need that are either out on loan or tucked away in a special reserve section. Spend a lot of time in the lending department, browse through the sections devoted to cooking and catering, business management and organisation and borrow the books which seem most helpful. You'll notice that library books have reference numbers printed on their spines. Those beginning with 640 deal with home management and organisation; cookery books begin with 641, accountancy 657 and starting your own business 658; so they shouldn't be difficult to find. When you are trying to work out which are the most helpful volumes in a bewildering collection, bear the following points in mind. It is a good idea to choose books that have been published comparatively recently. For instance, anything published in the fifties will now be wildly out of date and inappropriate unless it has been thoroughly and carefully revised within the past year or two (although some cookery books prove the exception to this rule). Books which have an index are easier to use and somehow inspire more confidence than those without. Good appendices of useful information – about further reading, helpful organisations, reference directories and so on – are also a valuable asset and will save you a great deal of personal research.

After exploring the lending library, you should find your way to the reference library. Tell the librarian what you are looking for and you should be given a lot of useful help and advice. The library will have full details of any societies or organisations that may be useful, and will have information on any classes being held – perhaps at the nearest college of technology – in cooking, catering and/or business management and accounting. There may also be short residential courses available. Alternatively, the librarian may refer you to the Citizens' Advice Bureau, which is always a treasure house of factual information, and they will know how you can get in touch with the Jobcentre, which may well be able to offer you retraining opportunities.

The library may also have a good periodicals section, and you'll find that not only specialist cookery journals but also practically every woman's general interest magazine devotes quite a lot of space to cookery. Often this concerns cooking for special events, for example, how to organise a buffet for twenty, a children's birthday party, an exotic dinner for up to a dozen or a large-scale barbecue or teenage disco, with lots of original and well-tested recipes. They also frequently have advice on growing and cooking for the freezer, bulk buying, decorative presentation, cake icing, as well as many other related topics.

If you come across an article that may be of use at some time, even though it has no immediate application, either get it photocopied (most large libraries have photocopying facilities these days) or buy your own copy of the magazine, cut out the relevant pages and file them away carefully so that they can easily be tracked down and used for future reference. In this way you can build up a useful library of your own which will, in time, hold the answer to practically every challenge with which you may be presented. It is wise, though, to try out every new dish or technique on your own family or circle of friends before you prepare it for a professional engagement. Even the most reliable of magazines has occasional problems with typesetting or subediting and makes errors with recommended weights and measures, misses out ingredients or omits a vital step in the list of instructions. Or it may be that your oven is rather idiosyncratic as regards temperature control – no two are ever exactly the same in my experience – and so the cooking time and heat may have to be adjusted accordingly. Sometimes a recipe that sounds absolutely delicious, and looks superb from the photographer's cleverly prepared illustration, can prove a great disappointment to the taste buds. So, don't cut corners or take risks. Everything should be thoroughly tried, tested and tasted first of all, and carefully costed too.

The same applies to television cookery courses. You can learn a lot from them, but all too often the expertise of the professional presenter makes some of the cooking look easier than it is. Practically no dish is foolproof, so you must always try them out yourself in a situation in which you have nothing to lose if something goes wrong.

Since there is no teacher as effective as personal experience, you might find it useful to try to work in some established field of catering for a short while before you are ready to take off on your own. It may not be easy to persuade a small home-based business to let you work with them for a time, while you learn from their experience and pick their brains, unless they are functioning well away from your area and can be convinced that you will not be setting up in direct competition. However, you could probably find part-time work in a restaurant, café or pub that serves meals so that you can observe the day-to-day running of the establishment, the standards of preparation and presentation and the methods, organisation and equipment needed to make the operation as smooth and efficient as possible, for the benefit of caterers and customers alike.

2
Basic Contacts

Any successful business depends upon good planning, organisation and budgeting, and this needs to start well before you begin your catering operation if you are to have a good chance of success.

Small Firms Service

The sensible first step is to make contact with the Small Firms Service. The skilled personnel who run it will probably have the answer to every question you need to ask. Just telephone them (you can get through to them free by dialling the operator and asking for Freefone 2444) and they will send you as much information as they think will be helpful in the first instance. When you have studied their leaflets very carefully, you can make an appointment to see one of their counsellors, whose own expertise, experience and local knowledge should enable him or her to explain any areas which may seem confusing. If you have really thought through the problems thoroughly and know beforehand exactly what questions you need to ask, you will only need a single session with them and all the advice you receive will be free, since the service is part of the Department of Industry and is paid for out of public money. If, however, you feel you need more advice – practical help, for instance, in making out a profit and loss type budget, or cash flow projections or creating your own simple accounting system – you can make follow-up appointments, and for these you will be charged a fee (£15 plus VAT for up to a full day's counselling at the time of writing). The Small Firms Service actively wants to help people like you and to make the public aware of its existence and the advice it has to offer. It frequently goes out to meet the public, setting up a mobile office in busy car parks, market squares, trade fairs and agricultural shows. If you see its caravan parked near you, don't be afraid to go in and have a chat, no matter how small and insignificant your catering idea may seem to you. You are almost certain to be received with a very warm welcome and with positive, practical encouragement.

After this important first step, you will probably need to make contact with a whole series of professional men and women who may have a part to play in your new venture.

Environmental Health Officer

Top of the list comes the environmental health officer, whom you will be able to track down at your nearest district council office. He will be very interested in the kitchen where you propose to do your cooking to make sure that it measures up to the standards of hygiene and cleanliness considered desirable. Remember that he is responsible for public health. Though many of us prepare food in kitchens that are not exactly spotless, that we may share with a family cat and a tribe of unhygienic children, that may boast a sink that could have been considered an antique in the days of Queen Victoria, if we are doing it for our own friends and families, and not for profit, that is considered our business. But when the health of the public may be at risk through unhygienic facilities it becomes a matter of public concern and you are governed by the Food Hygiene (General) Regulations. (You can get a copy of these from Her Majesty's Stationery Office or a simplified version from the Environmental Health Department.) It is important to realise that where conditions in any premises devoted to the preparation of food for the public present a risk of danger to health, the local authority may apply to the court for either a closure order or an emergency order which could prohibit the sale of food from the premises. So, listen carefully to the advice of your health officer and act upon it. Don't write him off as a bureaucratic busybody. It would be no joke to find yourself personally responsible for other people's suffering, whether it were caused by an outbreak of food poisoning or the spread of an infection or disease – and it wouldn't be very good for business either!

It is, of course, possible to go ahead without informing the environmental health officer about your activities, but you would be running a risk. Your business venture may come to his notice either through advertising or word of mouth. You may even find yourself providing the food for a function at which he is one of the guests. And then he'll probably pay you a visit without being invited. What could be much worse, if there is an outbreak of food poisoning and it is traced back to you, you could be in trouble.

My own environmental health officer, who was at pains to explain that he tried to be as co-operative, flexible and sympathetic as possible towards small-scale freelance enterprises and didn't expect them to measure up to the same rigorous standards which apply to restaurants and hotels, told me an interesting story of a case of food poisoning which caused local havoc but was, for many days, impossible to solve. All those who were ill, some of them very seriously, had had lunch in a certain pub. Yet the pub's kitchens, storage rooms and cooks were spotless and perfect. At last, after hours of exhaustive testing, analysis, questioning and culinary detective work, it came to light, quite by chance, that though most of the food was prepared on the premises, one special delicacy, the country pâté, was provided by a local freelance cook. No one had considered this little snippet of information worth mentioning before. Within hours the cook's kitchen was found to be the source of the food poisoning, but by then it had claimed a lot of victims.

Bank Manager

Your next visit should be to a friendly bank manager. You will need to open a new **business account**, which should be kept quite separate from your **personal account**, and the manager will need to know all the whys and wherefores of your proposed new venture. If you are running a small business, it is better to keep your account with a small local branch of a big bank. There you will be known and treated as an individual. In a large central city bank, which handles a lot of large and lucrative accounts, it is possible that your interests and problems may be considered comparatively trivial and you may not get the care and attention you need and deserve.

I discovered that it is preferable, if at all possible, to launch a business without asking for a loan from the bank. Loans cost a lot of money and, of course, you can only get one if you have some form of security to offer in return. The bank cannot risk losing its investment and should never be considered a philanthropic organisation. It is in the business of making money out of lending money.

It is also desirable, I think, to try to raise the money you need for any initial investment in equipment and food from your own financial resources – perhaps with a little help from partners, friends and family. But it is wise to arrange **overdraft facilities** with your bank manager. This means that you will be allowed to overdraw up to a certain pre-arranged limit whenever you need to. You will only pay interest on the actual amount you have overdrawn, not on a fixed sum, as is the case with a loan. Since your income and expenses may well fluctuate widely from day to day, depending upon whether you are buying a lot of food for a big event or receiving payment for a previous one, this could save you money while at the same time saving you from cash flow problems. You won't need to worry that more is going out than coming in, as long as you are sure that the tide will soon turn and more will come in than has been going out!

Never make the mistake of underestimating the financial outlay of putting on an event. For instance, you might be delighted to get a booking for a buffet supper for a hundred people. Perhaps you will decide that a reasonable charge would be £3 a head, and relish the thought of banking your cheque for £300. But – and it's a big but – before you receive your £300 you'll have to pay out approximately £100 in order to buy the basic food ingredients. You'll have to pay for petrol or hire some form of transport. You may need to buy extra equipment, as well as napkins, tin foil, kitchen paper or whatever. You may also have to pay wages for a certain amount of help. And then, after all that expense, it's quite possible that you may have to wait quite a long time for your customer to pay the bill. So you have to spend quite a lot of money before you actually make any – and that's why overdraft facilities are a comforting security blanket.

Be prepared for the fact that your bank manager may well ask you some searching questions about your business intentions. He or she will be interested in your experience, your potential customers, the competition you'll have to face from other caterers already established in the area, your overheads, your profit margin, your accounting method, your projected costings and so on. So do your homework properly (with the help of the advice you've gleaned from the Small Firms Service) before you keep your appointment, and make a good impression with your business-like approach. Certainly you must have a clear idea whether there really is a demand for the service you propose to offer or whether you can create the demand, how much it will cost you in the first instance and what financial return you can expect to gain.

When I began my own catering business I was given some very simple advice for which I was always grateful because it provided me with a certain amount of security and saved me a lot of sleepless nights. As well as opening a **current account**, it was suggested that I should have a **deposit account** containing a sum of about £400 as a 'sinking fund'. This was quite a small amount, but enough to reassure me that I could bale myself out if I ran into an emergency, such as a bad debt, an expensive breakage or a cash flow problem. A deposit account doesn't only bring peace of mind. It has the added advantage that it also earns interest, so it's well worth having. I only once had to dip into mine, in order to buy a larger and more efficient cooker, and I rapidly managed to replace the money I had taken out, but never a day passed without my being glad it was there, just in case.

Accountant

Your bank manager may suggest that you use the services of an accountant to advise you about keeping precise accounts, to keep your books in order, to prepare your accounts for the tax inspector and to help you with Value Added Tax and all its associated complications. VAT used to be a major headache for me because I had to charge it on food that was eaten on the premises, but not on food that was taken away. Since a lot of my customers used to say 'I'll have a piece of chocolate cake with my coffee now, and another to take home for tea – and will you add a couple of scones please . . .?' and then change their minds and eat one of their scones straight away, my calculations tended to be erratic, and my poor VAT inspector frequently felt a headache coming on when I tried to explain matters to him. Fortunately, VAT is no longer likely to be a problem for the beginner, since at the time of writing it is not applicable unless there is a turnover of £18,000.

The bank manager may recommend a particular accountant, but it is not wise to take his advice automatically without making a few further enquiries. It may be that he is trying to boost the business of one of his customers. Personal recommendation, from someone with direct experience of the service received, is usually more reliable.

The problem of whether or not to use an accountant needs a great deal of consideration, and your eventual decision will probably depend upon:

* the financial complexity of your business
* your own ability with figures
* what other financial advice or assistance is available to you

It is certainly true that astute accountants can save their customers a lot of money by knowing all about the various tax allowances they can claim. On the other hand, their charges are quite high, and unless you have a large turnover right from the beginning you may not feel able to cope with an annual accountancy fee of £100 plus. It may be better, in the early years at any rate, to teach yourself the rudiments of accountancy, either by going to classes or by studying the be-your-own-accountant books available in the library or provided by the Small Firms Service. You will also find that Part 1 of *Working for Yourself*, written by Godfrey Golzen and published by Kogan Page, is very clear and helpful about money matters. If you decide on this course, however, you should have an initial counselling session with an accountant before you get going. It will probably cost you less than you imagine, but it's wise to ask what the fee will be before you make the appointment.

Inspector of Taxes

As soon as you start work you must tell the local inspector of taxes (you'll find the address in the local telephone directory under 'Inland Revenue'). The easiest way to provide the information required is to acquire the Board of Inland Revenue's leaflet IR28 *Starting in Business* and fill in the form at the back. If you are changing from being an employee to being self-employed it will alter the basis on which you pay tax, and you will be taxed under Schedule D. This means that:

• you can claim all business expenses against tax
• your tax is paid at the end of the year rather than on the PAYE system

If you are not using an accountant, the tax inspector will give you information on allowable expenses that can be set against your earnings for tax purposes. For instance, if you are working from home you can include part of the cost of **heating, lighting, rent, rates and telephone.** You can also include **travel expenses** and the **business costs of running your car, postage** and **advertising.** Claiming proper allowances can save you pounds on your tax bill, so make sure you know exactly what you can include, then keep careful daily records of expenses, plus receipts and bills, in order to prove your point if requested. (It may seem like making a fuss, but you should always ask for a receipt when you make a purchase. If you pay by cheque the counterfoil will suffice.) It is not a good idea – though it might be tempting – to inflate your supposed expenses to wildly exaggerated proportions. The tax man is no fool; he knows roughly what is reasonable and what is a flight of fancy, and will almost certainly catch up with you in the end.

There is a middle course between paying for the services of a fully qualified accountant (who may be a member of either the Institute of Chartered Accountants or of the Association of Certified and Corporate Accountants) and doing the whole business yourself. Sometimes people advertise themselves as 'bookkeepers', or simply as 'accountants', without any letters after their name, and if you have a good unqualified person of this sort recommended to you he or she will probably be able to do a very adequate job in preparing tax returns for a small business. But do insist on that recommendation. Incompetence, inefficiency, dishonesty or any attempt at tax evasion could do you enormous damage.

Solicitor

Before you begin your new business, it is also wise to take legal advice, just to make sure that your venture is within the law. A solicitor may come across snags that you had not even considered. For instance, are you sure that you are allowed to carry on a business from your home? Some leasehold and tenancy agreements flatly forbid it, and this will need to be checked.

If your business is likely to disturb neighbours or cause a 'nuisance' by creating noise, smells, extra traffic, restriction of shared parking space, or if it means you will have to build an extension to your house to provide extra preparation, storage or cooking space, you must apply to the local authority for planning permission. And if that is granted, you may then discover that you are faced with higher rates because your home has become 'commercial premises'. Your solicitor will tell you whether you need to make an application for change of usage.

Many people carry on small businesses from their own homes quite unobtrusively without doing any harm at all and without attracting the attention of the local authority, and so they avoid the bother of red tape and the expense and delay which so often goes hand in hand with bureaucracy. You might decide to risk it, and you might get away with it, but it's just as well to have your neighbours on your side. For instance, if you are going to make a noise returning from a function late at night, or if you are expecting a lot of delivery vans or cars, a simple explanation can disarm criticism. A counsellor at the Citizens' Advice Bureau told me, 'The local authority often doesn't really want to know about tiny freelance business projects. They've got quite enough to do without ferreting out extra work for themselves. But then a neighbour takes the huff, gets uppity, decides to make trouble and put in a report. Then the council just has to get involved. You have no idea how often we get people coming in here asking for advice after this sort of row has upset the apple cart. If only people would learn to live together in a more friendly and co-operative way they would be much happier, and our job would be easier too.'

Your solicitor will also be able to advise you whether you should set yourself up as a **limited company**, a **sole trader** or a member of a **partnership**. A fourth, but less common, business arrangement is to establish a **workers' co-operative**. If your solicitor doesn't have any information about co-operatives, and many of them don't, you can get all the information you need by writing to both The Co-operative Development Agency, 20 Albert Embankment, London SE1 7TJ, and The Industrial Common Ownership Movement, The Corn Exchange, Leeds LS1 7BP. In a nutshell, a co-operative is a type of limited company owned and controlled equally by all its workforce in a completely democratic manner.

Limited Company
This may seem the best option in the first place because it has the great advantage of having, in law, a separate identity from the people who own it. In other words, if the company goes bankrupt it is the company's assets which are used to recompense the creditors, not the assets of the individual shareholders. If a sole trader or private partnership goes bankrupt, the creditors are entitled to get back what they are owed from the bankrupts' personal possessions – houses, cars, jewellery and so on. On the other hand, a limited company is hidebound by quite a lot of rules and regulations. It must, for example:

- have its annual accounts properly audited for the tax inspector
- make an annual return to the Registrar of Companies, listing all the shareholders and directors, any changes of ownership, a profit and loss account and a balance sheet

You can either buy a company ready-made and already registered by the registration agents who are selling it or you can begin your own company and build it out of nothing; whichever you choose to do, professional advice is absolutely vital because it is a tricky business.

Sole Trader
The main advantage of going into business as a sole trader is that you are your own boss, answerable to no one, a completely free

agent able to stamp your own image on your venture. The primary disadvantages are:

* it can be a lonely business having to shoulder all the responsibility, decision-making, planning and worry on your own
* you can lose a lot of work if you are ill, on holiday or have the offer of several bookings on the same day
* you may be short of funds if you only have your own financial resources to draw on

Partnership
This can be a splendid arrangement provided that the partners are well matched. As all the members of a partnership are personally liable for any debts incurred, even though they may have been the fault of only one partner, it is vital to choose someone with business acumen as well as a little money to invest in the firm. In fact, a partner needs much more than those two basic attributes, and the question of choosing people to work with is dealt with more thoroughly in chapter 3. When I was setting up my own catering business my solicitor gave me two pieces of advice. 'Don't saddle yourself with the complications of a limited company,' he said. 'Instead, watch your cash flow constantly and carefully and always have an emergency standby fund on deposit. Do find yourself one or two good partners, and choose them with even greater care than you would choose a marriage partner.' I took his advice and never had cause to regret it.

If you decide on a partnership, even if it's with your husband or wife, brother or sister, parent or child or lifelong friend or lover, it is still very important that your solicitor should draw up a formal partnership agreement. This should be worked out and worded in such a way that any areas of possible controversy can be solved by referring to it. Before you discuss it with your solicitor, each partner should make a list of the aspects of running a business that seem to him or her important enough to argue about, and some solution should be worked out theoretically and then incorporated into the document which should be considered sacrosanct. The sort of issues that it will cover are:

* which partner is responsible for what aspect of the business or are they all equally responsible for everything?

- are decisions to be reached by a majority vote or only when there is total unanimity?
- should all partners invest the same amount of money in the business?
- if not, do those who invest more money have more say in the management?
- how will the profits be divided? Will those who put more money in get more money out? Or will those who put in more time and effort receive more of the profits? Or will affairs be so arranged that an equal investment of time, money and effort will be required of each partner and the profit then shared equally?
- what will happen if one partner is ill or absent for any length of time or wishes to resign or dies?
- how will a new partner be admitted?
- when the business is eventually wound up, how will the assets be disposed of?

These are just a few of the questions which will need firm answers. Each separate partnership will no doubt come up with a different list, but the problems posed above should be enough to get you thinking along the right lines before you actually get down to the basic facts of the matter with your solicitor. Don't be misled into thinking that an insistence upon a legal agreement implies that you have any doubts about the integrity and good will of your potential partners or that it might damage friendships and other good long-standing relationships. On the contrary, it is more likely to safeguard them.

By now you should have made contact with: the **Small Firms Service**, the **environmental health officer**, a **bank manager**, an **accountant**, a **tax officer** and a **solicitor**. And you haven't begun to think about food yet! There are still one or two more contacts to be made before you move on to that stage. For instance, you need to go and talk to an insurance broker. If you don't know of one, your solicitor or accountant will almost certainly be able to advise you.

Insurance Broker

The ideal firm for you is one that is big enough to have a lot of insurance companies to choose from, to make sure you have the sort of cover you need, but not so big that it hasn't the time to take trouble over a small, individual client who will, to start with anyway, earn it only relatively small amounts of commission. When you outline your proposed business operation to your broker in detail he will be able to give you precise information about what sort of insurance you should have, but basically it will be similar to the list printed here:

* insurance of the premises in which you cook
* insurance of the equipment you use
* insurance of your stock (this can include not only foodstuffs, but also your contact book of names and addresses, your diary of future bookings, your recipe books and anything else that might have a bad effect on your business for some time if it happened to be destroyed)
* employer's liability if you employ staff
* public liability (in case you injure a member of the public or damage his premises) and third party coverage for your employees and/or partners
* insurance of yourself and your employees and/or partners against injury or accident
* insurance against losing your driving licence

Insurance is expensive. You may be tempted to think it is an expense you could risk doing without. If so, think again. You may go for years without making a claim and feel that you are wasting your money, but one bad accident can be totally catastrophic to the uninsured. And accidents can and do happen in the catering world. Many of the stories that assailed my ears while I was interviewing freelance cooks had their funny side, but at the time they were traumatic and expensive. For instance, there was Melanie, who tipped hot soup into the lap of a lady wearing a new Zandra Rhodes dress and had to pay for a replacement because it couldn't be dry cleaned. One of the students roped in to help Jill laid a very hot dish on a priceless and unprotected Sheraton table and the whole surface had to be repolished at Jill's expense. Julie tried to walk through closed French windows, carrying a tray laden with crystal glasses.

Moving from sunshine into shade, her eyes were momentarily dazzled, and she just didn't see the plate glass. Then there was Bill who booked a clown and fire-eater as the entertainment for a children's party. It was a brilliant idea and was wildly popular with the young guests – until the curtains caught fire and the party disintegrated into screaming chaos!

One of the most hilarious stories I came across, though it seemed terrible at the time, was the tragic tale of the ginger tom. Felicity had been booked to provide dinner for twelve in an elegant town apartment. She worked all day in her hostess's well-appointed kitchen, her only problem being that she had to share it with the large and handsome ginger tom for whom the kitchen was home. Stifling her doubts about what the environmental health officer would have to say about the proximity of food and domestic pets, she prepared a delicious crab salad, carried it to the dining room table and returned to the kitchen for plates and serving spoons. She got back to the dining room approximately five seconds too late to prevent Ginger from getting stuck into the crab and happily helping himself to a few generous mouthfuls from the centre of her artistically arranged master-piece. Picking him up in a frenzy, she banished him to the garden, then hastily forked up the crab and garnished it with sprigs of greenery to restore it to its former glory. All went well – at first. The guests devoured every morsel of the dish and declared it a triumph. Much later that evening, when the party was over and the washing up done, an exhausted Felicity opened the door to dump her debris in the dustbin and found Ginger on the step, stone-cold dead. 'The crab!' she screamed, and blurted out the whole story to her horrified client. After a panic-stricken debate, they decided they must tell the guests what had happened. Seafood, after all, has a notorious reputation for food poisoning. During a long, hard night, while Felicity had fitful dreams of being charged with mass murder, all twelve dinner party revellers went into hospital, had their stomachs pumped out and were eventually pronounced free from danger. Next morning a gentleman presented himself on the very doorstep from which Ginger's corpse had been gingerly removed. 'Awfully sorry,' he apologised to the ashen-faced hostess. 'I'm afraid I ran over your cat last night. On the road, just outside.

Killed it outright. I came to own up and apologise, but I could see through the window that you were having an awfully jolly party and I didn't want to spoil things. No hard feelings, I hope!'

Accidents can happen to the best of us. It's no good thinking 'but that would never happen to me'. Be prepared for the worst, hope for the best and, in the meantime, keep your insurance up to date. Don't do yourself the disservice of underinsuring either. You should check the value of your equipment every year and make sure that you are in line with current replacement values. Find a trustworthy broker – then trust him. Listen to his advice. This doesn't mean, of course, that you shouldn't read and consider your policies very carefully, paying special attention to the small print. You may not get all the right answers from your own examination, but at least it should put you in a position to ask the right questions.

National Insurance
If you are self-employed you will normally be required to pay Class 2 National Insurance contributions unless you have applied for and been granted exception because your earnings are below the exception limit. The exception limit tends to change from year to year, but you can find out what it is at present by consulting two leaflets, NI 208 and NI 27A. However, many people who are excepted choose to pay contributions voluntarily because of the benefits they confer. These include: basic **sickness benefit**, basic **retirement pension**, basic **widow's benefit**, **maternity grant**, basic **maternity allowance**, **child's special allowance** and **death grant.**

If your profits from self-employment are over a certain limit you may have to pay Class 4 contributions as well. Class 4 contributions are earnings related and are a percentage of your profit. The limits for liability change each year. To know more, you need leaflet NP 18 *Class 4 National Insurance Contributions.* If you are a married woman there are further complications and you need to study yet another leaflet, NI 1 *Married Women: Your National Insurance Position.* This is really a matter about which you need specialist advice, so do talk it over carefully at the DHSS office. If you still feel confused, the Citizens' Advice Bureau might well be able to clarify the issue.

Printer

There is one more person you should be making contact with at this stage, and that is the printer. You will almost certainly need to advertise your service in some way, probably in several ways, so it's a good idea to try to find out right from the beginning which forms of advertising work best, and how much they cost.

You'll very likely advertise in the local paper, but that may not be enough on its own. When I began my business I discovered that small printed handbills, size A5, were very effective, whether left in piles in public places like the library or the Tourist Information Office, fastened up in shop windows or slipped inside the local free advertising paper. (For more information on advertising see chapter 5.) But we also needed well-designed writing paper and cards with our own personal name and logo, something smart, distinctive and eye-catching that inspired confidence in our high standards. In any business, but perhaps particularly in self-catering, appearance and presentation are all important.

The prices, quality and efficiency of printers vary enormously, so again it's necessary to ask around and find out which ones in the area have a sound reputation for providing good work, at the right time and at the right price. If several printers are recommended, visit them all, compare the prices and delivery times they quote, see if they have any imaginative suggestions to make and, most important, have a careful look at examples of their work for other firms. Once you have found a good, stylish, competitive, reliable, co-operative printer, treasure him or her like gold dust. Such a paragon can be very hard to find.

All this early preparation will eventually pay dividends but will, nevertheless, take a few weeks. While you are fitting in interviews and working out costs and organisational details, you should also be getting out and about, meeting and talking to other people who are freelance caterers, watching them at work, even working with them if the opportunity presents itself, and finding out at first hand what their problems are and how they overcome them. Obviously no one is going to be very anxious to give you the benefit of their experience and expertise if they look upon you as a rival, attempting to muscle in on their field and steal away their customers. But once you have made it clear that you will be operating in another area or providing a different sort of service, they will probably enjoy the role of adviser and expert. In my early days I travelled miles just looking, listening and learning. No one ever refused to help. On the contrary, I found their kindness and co-operation quite overwhelming. Similarly, once I was established, many people came to see me, or wrote to me, about the pros and cons of setting up a small freelance business, and I was always delighted to help them if I could. It is quite astonishing how supportive other people can be if you approach them in the right way. The world of the small-scale, home-based, do-it-yourself organisation is light years removed from the ruthless cut and thrust of big business, and this communal goodwill is, for me, one of its main attractions and delights.

3
Finding Help

One of the most important decisions you will have to make when you are starting up your business is how other people will fit in with your plans. There is a large range of options at your disposal, and which one you choose will depend upon the:

- type of person you are
- sort of people you know who can help you
- choice of catering opportunities available to you
- amount of money you need to earn

Sole Trader

First, you need to know yourself. If you are strong-willed, have very positive views about exactly how things should be done and don't take kindly to either discussion or criticism, you should probably be in business on your own. It's possible that if you keep it small scale, are very capable and well organised and know exactly what you can manage comfortably and what would overextend you, you will be able to cope entirely on your own. For instance, with carefully planned bulk buying and cooking, a well-stocked freezer, efficient, labour-saving kitchen equipment and your own transport, you could do two or three small dinner parties each week or a large self-service buffet or children's party. You would, however, need sufficient energy, strength and self-discipline to keep yourself going even when you'd rather rest or do something else. Few people realise what an emotional strain it can be working solo. The fact is, it's comparatively easy to work within a discipline and structure laid down by someone else, clocking in at 9am and getting on with the job until 5pm, because it's what is expected of you and you are being paid for it. It's quite a different matter forcing yourself to go into the kitchen and work on your own when you are answerable to no one else. It's like running a demanding race without having a pace-maker to keep you up to the mark. It becomes especially difficult when you are not cooking for a special event with a deadline to meet, but are simply keeping up your reserves of food for when the next booking comes in. An empty diary has a strangely demoralising effect and can cause a kind of creeping paralysis, unless you are clever enough to recognise the symptoms and strong enough to do battle with them.

When I interviewed Jill, a single-handed, self-employed cook, she was going through a bad post-Christmas patch when no one seemed to need her skills. 'I've suddenly got very lazy,' she said. 'I'm just hanging around beside the telephone waiting for my next job to come in.' I suggested that this quiet period might be used fruitfully to stock up with pâtés and purées, sauces and soups, or to try out new recipes and techniques. 'You don't understand,' she said. 'When you're not working you begin to think you'll never work again. It's a very enervating experience. And in a weird way, you think that cooking for an engagement that hasn't been booked is tempting providence, and that you'll never be offered another one.'

Jill knew, of course, that she was being illogical and that her fears were unfounded. She had built up a sound reputation and an extensive range of contacts. Her skills were well known and respected, and she had two years of success behind her. What she was suffering from was the fact that in January and February her potential customers were hard up and suffering from a surfeit of Christmas and New Year festivities, and it would probably be March before they were ready for another batch of entertaining. She recognised this with her mind, but emotionally she found it difficult to accept and respond to the situation positively. She may well have been better off if she had had a partner or an assistant to keep her on her toes and boost her morale. It's a strange anomaly that in some ways one needs the help of other people even more in the quiet times than in the frantically busy ones, when the mind and body seem to respond to pressure by releasing extra reserves of energy.

Of course, it's perfectly possible to be in business on your own account but still call on other people for help. You can do this in several different ways, ranging from the informal and casual to the official. Although it's self-evident that cooking expertise is not the province of one sex, and that men and women can both excel in this field, it does seem that most small-scale freelance cooks are women, often still tied to family commitments. This has probably nothing to do with the nature of women or the essence of cooking; it is simply a matter of practical organisation. Many home-based women find that catering is an occupation in which they are experienced and one which they can pursue professionally without too much disruption of family life. If this applies to you, it's possible that you can get the support and extra help you need from within the family. They may be able to assist you with shopping, kitchen chores, transport, book-keeping, making up menus, serving, butling, or even the cooking itself if they are up to it. In fact, if they can feel involved and needed they are much more likely to be interested in your work than if they feel it is something that takes you away from them and occasionally relegates them to second place in your life. So, use your family, if they'll allow themselves to be used, but always pay them a reasonable rate for their labour, if they'll allow themselves to be paid. It can be a splendid way for teenagers to augment their pocket money, and even younger children, if carefully supervised, usually have something to offer which is worth a fair reward. How you organise your finances with your husband or partner is a much more complicated business but it does seem fair that joint earnings should go into a joint account. It's possible that he'll get a little annoyed if he does some of the work but all the financial return gets salted away into your own personal kitty. Talk it over beforehand and work out a solution that is acceptable to both of you if you want to avoid the wear and tear of financial squabbles.

Some women are forced, or prefer, to look for help outside the family, and ask their friends or neighbours to lend a hand while still keeping a firm hold on the reins themselves. They do the preliminary negotiating, plan the menu, mastermind the organisation, but other women step in to help with the actual cooking, preparation and serving. Obviously the friends usually expect to be paid, but in an informal set-up like this it's possible to play it by ear rather than according to any book of rules. Usually they are given a fair share of the profits, with the organiser keeping rather more for herself to compensate for the extra effort she expended, or they are paid a basic fee which bears some relation to the number of hours they have put in. If there's not sufficient profit to give them a reasonable return for their labour you have got your sums wrong and are:

- undercharging your customers
- overspending when doing your marketing
- making mistakes with your quantities and providing bigger portions of food or a greater variety of dishes than is economically viable

You must get your budgeting absolutely right from the beginning otherwise you'll get caught in a vicious spiral. Too many freelance cooks – and people who are providing other freelance services too – undercharge to start with. Since their prices are so cheap they get a lot of work. They work extremely hard, buoyed up with apparent success, only to find that they are not making any money at all. They may even be losing it. They press on a little while longer, imagining that they are simply experiencing teething troubles, and that these will vanish once they are properly established. Six months later, overworked and exhausted, they are still out of pocket. Desperation, or a good accountant, decrees that they must charge substantially more if they are to survive. They put their prices up – and instantly lose clients. 'It was just a con,' their clients say. 'They deliberately kept their prices low in the first place to get our custom, and when we stood by them and gave them bookings and recommended them to our friends they then decided they could charge the earth.' And they take their business elsewhere. Within a year or so the brave new catering venture has foundered – and all because the original arithmetic was wrong. To find out how to get it right see chapter 7 on marketing.

Sometimes it's easier to keep friendships and business activities separate, if you want both to flourish. In this case you can still get help by looking for people in your area who have the time and skill to help you on a casual basis. They won't necessarily be difficult to find. If you ask around you may well discover that there are good cooks living nearby who would be glad to earn an extra penny or two by providing you with made-up dishes that they do well and will fit in easily with your menu planning. When I ran a village café I had two outworkers of this type. One provided us with three separate items, savoury flans, fruit cake and shortbread, all of which were so excellent and so greatly appreciated by our customers that we got quite a name for them and people came out of their way to eat them on the premises or to buy them to take away. The other cook was able to bake perfect fatless sponges, and they too had their devoted followers. In both cases we provided the ingredients, picked up the goods once or twice a week and paid our workers each month for the number of hours they had recorded in the notebooks we gave them, plus an extra amount for fuel or power. They didn't make a lot of money out of the deal and neither did we, but they enjoyed a pleasant pocket money hobby and an extra interest, and we enhanced our reputation. Many of those who came for cake and shortbread also had cream teas or tea, toast and sandwiches, on which we were able to gain a higher profit margin.

Once the business gets larger and more firmly established, you may feel the need for a regular workforce, in which case you can employ people properly, either full-time or part-time. There are difficulties though. You may find yourself faced with the complications of National Insurance and a mass of legislation protecting employees. Many employers will tell you that the law favours the employees at their expense, and that it's only when you get yourself a paid staff that your troubles really begin. This is probably an exaggeration. Nevertheless, before you rush off and hire staff ask yourself the following questions:

- do I really need them and is there enough work to keep them busy on a regular basis?
- can I afford to pay them the going rate for the job and their National Insurance, even during slack periods?
- do I know exactly what I want them to do?
- am I sure that I am able to judge their competency, honesty and reliability before I actually employ them? (If you have to get rid of them, they may be able to claim unfair dismissal)

The main items you need to know before you acquire an employee are briefly outlined in the following pages. There should be enough information here to help you decide whether you should go ahead and employ staff or whether you could find some other way of getting the help you need.

Contract of Employment

If an employee is going to work for you for sixteen hours or more per week, he or she must have a written contract of employment which lays down exactly the conditions that have been agreed between you. These will include: **hours of work**, **holidays** and **holiday pay**, **duties**, the **rate of pay**, and whether it is due weekly or monthly, **sick pay**, **pension**, notice of **termination of employment** required by both parties, **disciplinary rules** and **grievance procedures**.

Unfair Dismissal

Every employee, including all those who work for you for more than sixteen hours a week in other than a freelance capacity, and who have been employed by you for fifty-two weeks or more (104 weeks or more in the case of a new business) must be given a written reason if you wish to dismiss him or her. He or she must also be given one week's notice, or payment in lieu, if he or she has been with you for four weeks or more and, after two years, one week's notice for every year of employment. Fair grounds for dismissal are: **misconduct**, **incompetence** or **redundancy**. That sounds fine, but dismissed employees often tend to feel that your grounds for terminating their employment are unfair, and can take their cases before an industrial tribunal. So you must be able to prove your point and show that you have acted reasonably before coming to the crunch of the actual dismissal.

Misconduct

For instance, in cases of real misconduct you should give the employee not less than three written warnings, stating what he or she is doing wrong, advising him or her to put it right and explaining what will happen if the warnings are ignored.

Incompetence

The matter of incompetence is usually more difficult to prove and you have to tread very carefully or you may find the tribunal will back the employee and not you. The penalties for losing an unfair dismissal case can be devastatingly expensive, so you would be wise to consult a solicitor before you take action.

Redundancy

This occurs when jobs are lost through a business closing down or having to cut back on its workforce. If an employee has been employed for two years or more he or she will be entitled to redundancy pay worked out on a basis of length of service and salary scale. About half of this can be claimed back from the Department of Employment but you must give the Department written notice in advance.

Maternity Leave

It can also be tricky to employ a woman who may have a baby. If she works until eleven weeks before the birth and has been employed by you for two years or more, she is entitled to take off forty weeks and then return to work. If you find a replacement for her you must be very careful because, unless you notify the new employee in writing that the appointment is only temporary and give notice when it is coming to an end, the replacement can sue you for unfair dismissal!

Income Tax and National Insurance

The other complicated responsibility of being an employer is that it is your job to deduct Income Tax and National Insurance contributions under the Pay As You Earn (PAYE) arrangements, and to account for them to the collector of taxes. You can find out more about this by asking for copies of the employers' guides to PAYE and National Insurance (leaflets P7 and NP 15) at your local tax office. If your employees earn less than £32.50 a week (as of April 1983), they are not liable for National Insurance contributions. If they earn more than this, it is your job to pay both the employer's and the employees' contributions, but you are entitled to deduct the latter from their earnings. The

Department of Health and Social Security will be able to explain all this to you.

Food Hygiene Regulations

As an employer you are also responsible for making sure that your employees observe the Food Hygiene Regulations, and you could be in trouble with the law if you neglect to do so. One or two of the things you must bear in mind on their behalf are given below, taken from The Food Hygiene (General) Regulations 1970. Of course, they apply to you too.

Personal Hygiene

All food handlers, other than waiters and those engaged only in handling raw vegetables, intoxicating liquor or soft drinks, must wear clean and washable overclothing, and anyone who carries meat which is liable to come into contact with the neck or head must wear a clean and washable neck and head covering. Food handlers must:

- keep themselves clean
- keep their clothing or overclothing clean
- keep any exposed cut or abrasion covered with a suitable waterproof dressing
- refrain from the use of snuff, tobacco or other smoking mixture in any food room where there is open food
- refrain from spitting

Outdoor or other clothing and footwear must not be kept in any food room where open food is handled except in closed locker accommodation.

If a food handler becomes aware that he is suffering from, or is a carrier of, typhoid, paratyphoid or any other salmonella infection or amoebic or bacillary dysentery or any staphylococcal infection which is likely to cause food poisoning, he must inform the owner of the business who must then notify the appropriate medical officer for the district.

Food

Food must not be exposed to any risk of contamination and food handlers must ensure that:

- unfit food is kept apart from other food
- unprotected food is not displayed lower than eighteen inches from the ground in any forecourt or yard
- no animal feed is stored in open containers in any food room

Food handlers must not:

- carry any food in a container with any article from which there is a risk of contamination
- allow any live animal or live poultry to come into contact with food
- use any container or wrapping material for food which is liable to contaminate the food

(Extracted from The Food Hygiene (General) Regulations 1970.)

It may be that after you have considered all this you will come to the conclusion that life would be considerably easier if you forgot about the idea of having paid employees and relied instead upon casual labour or part-timers who work for less than sixteen hours a week, the stipulated minimum above which a contract of employment is necessary. When you are thoroughly established and successful you can always review the situation again, and it's possible that by then the benefits may outweigh the disadvantages.

Partnership

Alternatively, you could form a partnership and forgo the advantages of being your own boss for the security and moral support of having other people to share the worry, work and responsibility. As already suggested, it is always wise to have a legally drawn-up partnership agreement as a good insurance against argument, chaos and the possible breakdown of erstwhile happy relationships.

Before you get to that stage you should work out, with immense care and thought, how many partners you need and exactly what sort of person you are looking for. This will depend, of course, on what role your partner is going to play in the running of the business. Perhaps your main need is for an injection of cash. In that case you will have to agree about what perks go with the investment. Will he or she be simply a 'sleeping partner' or will the money invested give the investor the right to a say in how your catering operation should work? Will the partner actually take a share of the practical work or will he or she simply be allocated a proportion of the profits if and when any are made?

Perhaps your need is for a particular cooking skill. If you are a dab hand at soups, pâtés and casseroles, but couldn't make a quiche lorraine to save your life, you may need a good pastry cook. If you excel in English cooking but find yourself faced with a demand for Continental dishes, perhaps you should search for someone with an expertise in French cuisine. If you are without parallel at providing elegant candle-lit dinners for four, but are sent screaming up the wall by a group of forty mixed infants avid for jelly, sausages and strawberry ice-cream, you should be looking for an experienced mum with several years of children's parties behind her. In other words, if it's versatility you're after, you need someone with skills to complement your own rather than duplicate them. If you're planning to specialise, instead of offering a whole range of catering services, you won't need such a variety of talents.

Probably the best partnerships are those in which the partners can turn their hand to practically anything if need be, though inevitably some will have more talent in certain areas than others. The supreme advantage of this situation is that if one partner is ill, on holiday or entangled with other commitments, the others can carry on regardless, fulfilling their engagements without loss of either good will or hard cash.

Even more important than either money or cooking skill is a potential partner's temperament. This cannot be emphasised too strongly. If you are working with a partner with whom you don't see eye to eye, who irritates you or lets you down, any joy or satisfaction you may find in your business will rapidly evaporate in daily annoyances, grievances and petty rows. The ideal partner is not necessarily a friend or someone with whom you have a close personal relationship. Often this causes more problems than it solves. An acquaintance with whom you can develop a comfortable but purely business-like relationship may well be a better bet.

Having worked for seven years with an ideal partner, with whom I had occasional differences of opinion but never a cross word, and with whom I shared a certain amount of worry, a great deal of laughter and an enormous burden of hard work, I would list the qualities required of a perfect partner as follows: **unflappability**, **commonsense** and a **level-headed approach** to problems, **cheerfulness**, a **pleasant manner** and a **sense of humour**, **energy**, **good health** and a **capacity for hard work**, **commitment** and **consideration** for other people, **efficiency** in cookery, planning, organisation or financial administration, but preferably all four, **total reliability** and sufficient **time** available for the job.

If you can find a person like this, you're in luck. If you can find two, count your blessings. Some of the groups I spoke to were absolutely adamant that a partnership of three was an ideal number, though many had casual cooks and helpers they could call upon to augment their forces if they were particularly busy with a series of bookings or had an especially large or demanding function to cater for. A combination of three active and like-minded partners can have several things to commend it:

- it can survive a period when one of the group is unavailable, so that all can have proper holidays, adequate time off and feel free of any notion of guilt or inadequacy if events overtake them and they are unable to fulfil their commitments
- decision-making is sometimes simplified if there is an odd number of people involved so that one can always have the casting vote
- three partners means that there are three kitchens to draw on, three sets of equipment, three lots of cookery books and tried and tested recipes and, with luck, three lots of transport
- three people working together in harmony, and helping and supporting each other properly, means that there is more energy, morale boosting and mutual encouragement to trigger off higher levels of achievement and creativity

On the other hand, a partnership of two, if they are a really well-matched couple, can work extraordinarily well and cut out a lot of time-consuming debate because it often happens that in a threesome there is an odd one out who can cause immense difficulties. Having worked first with two partners and then with only one, my experience was that the twosome was much more efficient and easy to manage.

Since the choice of partner is of such vital consequence, it is sensible to move into it cautiously. First of all, think through all the possibilities very carefully before you decide who to approach. Secondly, always insist on starting off with a trial three-month period from which you can both withdraw at the end without any ill feeling or loss of face. If your potential partner hasn't proved as effective in practice as seemed likely, be brave, opt out and look again until the right person is found.

Co-operatives

Co-operatives work on similar lines to partnerships except that they are based on totally democratic principles, with equal rights, responsibilities and shared work and profits (or losses) for all concerned.

I interviewed many co-operative groups and found that, though several had organised themselves in different ways, they all had one thing in common. Decision-making was taken by the group, in group meetings, that could be lengthy and exhausting affairs because they continued until unanimous agreement was reached, no matter how long the process took. 'Our get-it-off-your-chest meetings', they were called by one particularly effective and dedicated co-operative in the North East of England. 'We all acknowledge that we have the right, the duty, to say exactly what we think. All the grievances, worries, niggles, discontents are brought out for an airing. It hurts. There are sometimes tears. But we have a pact that the meeting will not end until the differences are resolved, and no one is allowed to harbour a grudge or nurse a personal resentment.' This particular group ran a little 'homemade' shop, and had evolved a system in which everyone could do everything. They were convinced that it was the only way they could all understand the minutiae of their business and sympathise and help with each other's problems and difficulties. They worked on a monthly cycle. For one month one person was responsible for marketing, another for cooking, another for looking after the books, another for keeping their premises spotless – and that included cleaning the loos and sluicing down the backyard as well as scrubbing shelves, cleaning windows and so forth – and another for looking after the eleven children they shared between them, ferrying them back and forth to school, preparing their lunch and tea, keeping them occupied until the shop closed and all day during the holidays, being totally responsible for their entertainment and welfare. Many people say that co-operatives can't work for long, that every group needs a leader, and that too much talk wastes time and energy and solves nothing. In my experience, if they are made up of the right mix of people, and those people are totally dedicated to making a success of a co-operative venture, it can be a system which reaps rewards not only in terms of business profits, but also in personal satisfaction, understanding and growth.

4
Kitchen Layout and Equipment

It is impossible to generalise in a book of this nature about what sort of kitchen layout and equipment is vital to the freelance caterer, since it is intrinsically connected with the sort of catering you plan to provide. If, for instance, you are aiming at a complete range, from large children's parties to small sophisticated dinners, you will obviously need a very well-planned, well-equipped work space. Your requirements will also depend upon whether you are working single-handed or as one of a group, sharing the equipment available, though even in a group there must be a certain amount of duplication. For instance, if there are three of you, and you have to rattle off two hundred vol-au-vents, you are all going to need rolling pins, though you may get away with one shared deep freeze.

Your first job, if you can afford it, is to try to get your kitchen as well fitted as possible as far as its permanent features are concerned. A double sink with double drainers is ideal, but your environmental health officer may also insist on a separate hand basin so that you don't wash yourself and dispose of your germs in a sink which is used either for food preparation or dish washing.

If money is available, a good dish washer will save you hours of work. Make sure that you maintain it properly though; follow the manufacturer's instructions religiously and keep it topped up with the recommended detergent, salt, rinse-aid or whatever else is required, otherwise you won't get your dishes as clean and sparkling as you can do by washing them by hand.

You will also need as much cupboard and/or shelf space as possible. Whether you choose cupboards or shelves or a combination of the two is a matter of personal preference. Shelves tend to be more convenient as everything on them is

instantly visible and therefore easily found, and the bother of
opening and closing doors is eliminated. However, the objects on
them do attract dirt, dust and grease, especially in a kitchen
where a great deal of cooking is done. Cupboards keep things
cleaner, but the contents are less accessible, especially if they are
well packed, and every extraction involves a great deal of
rummaging around and reorganisation. (Incidentally, it makes
life easier if you keep your catering foodstuffs in a cupboard
quite separate from your family groceries and provisions; it will
also help to get your marketing and budgeting on a proper
business footing.)

Try to have your cupboards and shelves within comfortable
reach. It is no joke, when you are in a hurry and perhaps have
floury or sticky hands, to have to find a chair to perch on in order
to reach down some vital ingredient from a shelf way above your
head. Of course, all vital ingredients should have been assembled
before the cooking began, but none of us is perfect and we all
make this mistake! Teetering around on chairs can be a safety
hazard too. Thousands of accidents happen in the kitchen during
an average year and a lot of them are due to falls, so always be on
your guard against this danger. If you can't avoid having some of
your cupboards out of reach, be sufficiently well organised to use
them only for the things that are used only rarely, and try not to
delve into them in a hurry.

On the subject of kitchen safety, you really do need to have a
fire extinguisher mounted on the wall in an easily accessible
place. Make sure, as soon as you acquire it, that you know
exactly how to use it in an emergency and won't bungle it in a
state of panic. There'll be no time for a leisurely perusal of the
instructions if you suddenly find yourself faced with a cooker
fire.

As well as ample storage, adequate working surfaces are
important too. You need lots of these, and they should be
covered with a thoroughly hygienic material such as laminated
plastic so that they can be easily and effectively cleaned. Try not
to keep lots of things standing around on the surfaces when
you're not working. You will just have to clear them all away
when you begin to cook and, since your cupboards are probably
bulging at the seams, the extra bits and pieces are likely to end up

on the floor where they stand a high chance of tripping you up or getting broken.

Flooring needs consideration too. Again, this is one of the things that your friendly environmental health officer is going to be interested in. It needs to be: **easily cleanable** and **non-slippery**. Scatter rugs on wooden boards are not advisable, though they may look very attractive. Cork tiles, linoleum tiles or quarry tiles, very thoroughly sealed with several coats of a patent sealing fluid, are a good idea. Any surface that has chinks or crannies, like strips of linoleum that aren't properly joined together, can harbour particles of food that will eventually attract bugs, mice or lice, or all three. It makes sense, if you are planning to change your kitchen flooring, to telephone the Environmental Health Department beforehand to see what they recommend as the most hygienic solution to the problem. (There's no need to confess that you're cooking professionally if you don't want to. Ordinary members of the public have a vested interest in health and cleanliness too.) If you get the right advice at the outset you may save yourself a lot of time and money later on.

You will also require as many power points as possible scattered around the kitchen, preferably at working surface level. You don't want to be scrabbling around on your hands and knees every time you have to switch on your electric mixer. Never underestimate the number of electric sockets you need. The electrical equipment I have in my kitchen at this moment is as follows: **extractor fan, cooker, fridge, freezer, slow cooker, toaster, kettle, sandwich maker, coffee grinder, ice-cream maker, coffee percolator, food mixer** and **liquidiser, iron, heated airing rack, dish washer, washing machine** and **radio.** If I were more gadget conscious or had different dietary preferences, I might add: **hot trolley, frying pan, deep fat fryer, carving knife, cream maker** and so on.

They all have to be plugged in somewhere, so don't stint. Single sockets with multiple adaptors can be dangerous, and it's inconvenient and time-consuming to have to keep unplugging one piece of equipment in order to plug in another. I also know, from bitter experience, that in the heat of the moment it's possible to get in a muddle over what you are actually connecting. I still remember with mortification the day I switched on my slow cooker before I left home, shortly after breakfast, and returned at six o'clock that evening expecting to be greeted by the wonderful welcoming aroma of beef casserole, only to discover that the toaster had been plugged in instead and the beef was, naturally enough, still raw. We dined that night, sadly, on hamburgers – but I had learned a useful lesson.

Though the smell of food cooking is usually delicious, especially when prepared by a clever cook, you can have too much of a good thing. Consequently, a powerful extractor fan will make your house a happier place to live in. It not only gets rid of smells, it also carries away grease-laden fumes, leaving you with a cleaner and sweeter kitchen that doesn't need redecorating so often.

You will also find that adequate and well-placed lighting is very important to your feeling of health and well-being, especially if you have to do some of your cooking in the evening. There should be a strip light or spot light over every working area, otherwise you will find yourself suffering from eye-strain or headaches. A centrally placed ceiling light unfortunately only casts distracting shadows. It may be the height of luxury, but it's also very useful to have lights inside cupboards as well. I can't be the only cook in the land who has had to rummage around in a low cupboard with a torch, or who has emerged triumphant after five frantic minutes of searching, clutching the desired bottle of vanilla essence – only to discover, too late, that it was actually peppermint flavouring!

The message of this section of the chapter is that, when you're working and wherever you're working, physical comfort and convenience are all important. So don't forget heat. We tend to think that as the oven is so often on, and because the kitchen is not normally a place where we sit and relax, we don't need to make any special efforts to warm it properly. Wrong! My first kitchen, in a quaint Cornish cottage, had a stone-flagged floor and a tiny electric fan heater. I spent my winters there suffering agonies from chilblains in both toes and fingers. My next kitchen was huge and had a high ceiling. It faced north, had tiny windows which never caught the sun and only one small storage heater, tucked away at the end of it. I avoided chilblains – but I also avoided the kitchen whenever I possibly could, except in the heat of high summer. The lesson is loud and clear. Find the best heating you can afford, make sure it is safe (not a free-standing gas or paraffin heater and not a little electric fire with a lethal lead just waiting to trip you up) and insist that your work space is comfortably warm. After all, if you worked in a shop or factory you would find that there were laws to protect your physical comfort, so there's no reason at all why you shouldn't insist on the same protection in your kitchen. What's more, you can legitimately claim an allowance for heating when you make your tax return.

Finally, if you are able to do any reorganisation of your kitchen before you start your new business, try to work out the most sensible place to put things. Obviously you should keep the fridge and deep freeze well away from the oven; food storage should be near work surfaces, and there should be a work surface beside the cooker. The less tramping about you have to do from fridge to cupboard to worktop to cooker to worktop again, the less exhausted you will get. A great deal of research has gone into planning the ideal working arrangement for a kitchen, the main aim being to eliminate unnecessary or difficult movements. It has been estimated that, on average, a full-time housewife spends up to eight hours a day in the kitchen and can travel up to three miles while she's there. The statistics are probably even more horrifying for a freelance cook.

There are three major focal points within any kitchen: **food storage**, the **sink** (the busiest place of all) and **cooking facilities**. Ideally, the walking distance between these three main areas should not be more than six metres. They should be linked by secondary areas, working surfaces, cupboards and drawers. The position of the worktops is vital. For example, there should be:

* one near the refrigerator or larder, food cupboards and deep freeze so that it's easy to unload shopping and put it away rapidly
* two near the sink, where vegetables and salads can be prepared, and crockery, cutlery and pans stacked for washing and draining (this could be a double drainer or a drainer and worktop on either side of the sink)

- two near the cooker, preferably one on either side, for preparing food for cooking and serving, and for placing hot dishes (obviously these should be heat-resistant)

Included here are several kitchen plans so that you can choose for yourself what fits in most easily with the arrangement you already have, and the size and shape of your kitchen. Almost certainly it will conform to one of six basic layouts: the **one-wall 'single line' kitchen**, the **galley kitchen**, the **U-shaped kitchen**, the **L-shaped kitchen**, the **F-shaped kitchen** or the **island site kitchen**. The diagrams opposite demonstrate possible plans.

Food Preparation and Storage

So much for kitchen planning. The next concern is kitchen equipment. You can, in fact, get away with very little, but if you're really looking upon this as a serious venture and not just a pleasant hobby, you will need:

- large deep freeze for long-term storage
- capacious refrigerator for short-term storage
- large cooker, preferably with a double oven
- set of large pans, including a three-gallon preserving pan, which you will probably use not for preserving, but mainly for its capacity. (There's no need to have a great many pans. It's probable that the space on the top of your cooker is limited, as is the area of your work surface and storage space, so it's better to have a few good pans which are used often and washed up straight away rather than investing a lot of money in a dozen or so which spend most of their time standing about dirty on your draining board or cluttering up your cupboard)
- casserole dishes
- pâté dishes, which come very cheap when bought full of pâté
- automatic mixer/blender/beater/liquidiser; in fact, two liquidisers would be handy since their use is so versatile, being invaluable for sweets and savouries, soups and sauces, solids and drinks

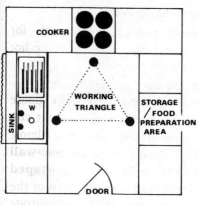

1. U-shaped

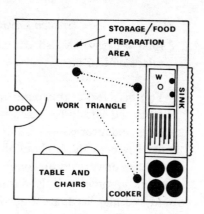

2. L-shaped

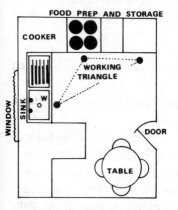

3. F-shaped

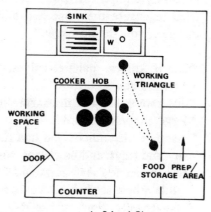

4. Island Site

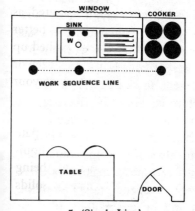

5. 'Single Line'

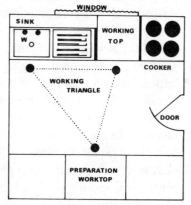

6. Galley

- food processor for shredding or chopping large quantities of salads and so on

You may feel at this point that you have managed to cook for friends and family for years without needing fussy gadgets like mixers and processors but, if you are to be business-like, you must begin to think about the value of your time. It is not a worthless or very cheap commodity. Time is worth money. Consequently, time- and labour-saving devices, if conscientiously used and mastered, are a good investment.

You will be relieved to know that the above list represents the most expensive, sophisticated and space-consuming part of your necessary equipment. But there are many other items you will need to ensure the smooth running of your organisation. For instance, you should have:

- sharp knives, palette knives, fish slices, wooden spoons, spatulas and so on
- accurate scales and measuring jugs
- large chopping boards
- standard size quiche and flan tins, cake tins, bun tins, baking tins and trays, and bowls and basins of various sizes. If you are to have some cakes, tarts and flans ready to go into the oven while others are baking, you will need a considerable quantity of ovenware. Some cooks rely heavily on disposable tin foil containers both for cooking and freezing, but this does add considerably to the expense, even though they can usually be washed and re-used a few times (needless to say, if you choose to pay out the extra cash for disposable containers you must include this item of expenditure when you are working out your budget and preparing to present your bill)
- lidded plastic containers of different shapes and sizes for the storage of basic ingredients before cooking, for freezing, for keeping airtight after cooking and for transporting food from home to the place where it is to be eaten. Spills or breakages en route can spell disaster. Note that ice-cream containers, margarine tubs, cream or yoghurt cartons all make invaluable containers, and it's rarely necessary to spend money on these, but they must have tight lids and be unspillable. It's also

important to label containers with contents and date, whether you are storing them in a cupboard or deep freeze or stacking them into the boot of your car. This will save hours of confused searching in the long run, and if you're working with other people it will make it much easier for them to get on, on their own initiative, without having to ask you for instructions all the time

- cling film and foil. Though foil is expensive it can be wiped clean and used again if it doesn't get too messy or tattered, so treat it carefully and save the pennies
- tea towels, paper towels and wiping-up cloths to help you clean up as you go and save yourself the more difficult and time-consuming task of dealing with burnt-on or congealed food or dried-up spillage

Three items which caused a lot of controversy among the cooks I interviewed, but which I find invaluable are: a **pressure cooker**, a **slow cooker** and an **ice-cream maker** which works inside the deep freeze. If you want to make really special ice-creams and frozen puddings, the sort of dish that gets you a reputation for having a particular expertise not found among other caterers, read *Making Ice-Cream and Cold Sweets* by Bee Nilson, published in paperback by Mayflower, Granada. It's full of mouth-watering possibilities.

Just as I am devoted to my ice-cream maker, I find my pressure cooker and slow cooker essential parts of my equipment, and they are in constant use. I was given my pressure cooker as a wedding present many years ago and would now feel totally lost without it. My slow cooker is a much more recent acquisition but it has been one of my most treasured possessions ever since it took up residence in my kitchen. It has the knack of bringing out the most superb flavours from the dishes I make in it, it helps me organise my time and maintain my peace of mind by keeping food hot for as long as necessary without ever over-cooking it, and uses the bare minimum of electricity.

However, other cooks I have talked to insist that ice-cream makers, pressure cookers and slow cookers are quite unnecessary, and even some of those who possessed them said that they very rarely used them. Obviously these are items about which each individual has to make up his or her own mind, but they are certainly worth considering and trying out, if you have the opportunity. Perhaps you could borrow one from a friend for a week's trial. If so, two more books will help you gain the most benefit from the trial period: *Pressure Cooking Day by Day* by Kathleen Broughton, published by Pan, and *Leave it to Cook* by Stella Atterbury, published by Penguin.

Food Presentation

Your food must look good as well as taste good and be served at the right temperature if it is going to give the maximum pleasure and satisfaction. Just as white wine should be served pleasantly chilled and red wine at room temperature, so cold food should remain cold and hot food hot if it is to be thoroughly enjoyed. This may sound like a truism and hardly worth mentioning, but it is amazing how often I have eaten rather warm cucumber sandwiches and rather cold moussaka, not because the caterers lacked skill or were using the wrong ingredients but because they hadn't thought out their problems of organisation and presentation carefully. One tends to forget, when planning a wedding, that temperatures in a marquee can soar to the nineties and that the food will wilt as surely as the guests. And it's not always remembered that if the kitchen happens to be a long way away from the dining room where you are trying to serve a hot dinner on a cold winter's night the food will almost certainly suffer from a chill during the journey!

To help you keep food hot, you will need: a **heated trolley** or **tray**, preferably with a cupboard below, which can keep a whole meal hot and succulent for two hours without spoiling, and, our old friend, a **slow cooker** or **hot pot**. To keep food either hot or cold, there are available on the market a whole range of: **insulated dishes** and **Thermos containers**. Have a look round a large department store with a good range of camping or picnic equipment and work out how you could use their wares to your own advantage.

For attractive visual presentation, you need a quantity of large and elegant **serving plates, trays or platters**. These can be hired but the cost may add unnervingly to your overheads, so it's a good idea to collect a supply of your own. This need not be as expensive as you fear if you begin to haunt jumble sales, junk shops and market stalls, but not antique shops, which tend to inflate their prices. Sometimes it's also possible to pick up bargains at house clearance or closing down sales, or auctions of bankrupt stock, if you have time to rummage and explore thoroughly before the bidding begins.

If you are frequently required to provide flower decorations, keep your eyes open for **vases** or other suitable containers. Remember that a good imaginative eye can save you a large amount of money. Flowers can look good in the most unlikely receptacles from dyed egg shells to old-fashioned tea pots. Think also about jars and jugs, bottles, mugs and tankards, pretty cups and saucers, little wickerwork baskets, wine glasses and goblets, decorated yoghurt cartons, tin cans and sea shells – the possibilities are limitless.

A large supply of **napkins and doilies** also helps to give a finishing touch. Buy them in bulk at your Cash and Carry, and choose good quality products in tasteful and neutral colours. Keep to the same basic colour scheme, something like beige or brown, that will go with anything, otherwise you'll find yourself left with lots of bits and pieces that you can't use up and that is money wasted.

Some customers will want you to provide **glasses, cutlery and crockery** if they are having a large party which is beyond their normal household resources. If you make enquiries of your local commercial caterer you'll probably find that he or she will offer to hire you whatever you need for the apparently minimal cost of 5p per item. That sounds fine – until you do your sums. Suppose you are putting on a relatively modest buffet for twenty people. For that you'll need a minimum of twenty plates, twenty bowls or dishes, twenty glasses, forty knives, twenty forks and spoons, twenty serving spoons. Probably much more. So you're nearly up to £10 before you've even started. And you've got the extra work and expense of picking up the items before the party and returning them afterwards, so petrol and the wear and tear on your car should be included. If you can afford it, therefore, and (this is very important) if you have adequate storage space, it makes better sense to buy your own, gradually building up an adequate supply. Choose a simple design which can easily be replaced or added to, probably made by an established firm which is not liable to go out of business or change its range rapidly. If you're providing your own glasses, make absolutely sure that they're tough, machine washable, cheap and easily replaced. (Many of the cooks I spoke to were reluctant to have anything to do with providing wine and always left that to the party host. However, there is no reason, if you feel yourself to be a reasonable judge of wine and can get it at a good price, why you shouldn't buy two or three cases and include the cost of the wine along with the food in the overall charge; this can add considerably to your profit margin.)

There is an alternative to either hiring or buying all the equipment you need for a large engagement, and that is to come to some mutually reciprocal agreement with other small-scale catering enterprises in your neighbourhood. Again and again I was told of useful arrangements whereby one cook might lend her large white tablecloths to another on the understanding that she would be able to borrow a set of avocado dishes when she needed them, or of large casseroles that spent their lives in perpetual motion, circulating around a ten-mile radius of freelance activities, or of silver candlesticks that had graced more dining tables in the southern counties than the most popular socialite. This friendly co-operation is an attractive notion, much more so than the cut-throat rivalry of many large firms. Its only disadvantage is that during late spring and summer, when there are lots of wedding parties, or during the Christmas festivities, you may all be working at full stretch and quite unable to come to each other's assistance.

If you have to hire cutlery and crockery, or if you have to borrow money in the first instance to buy a supply of your own and then pay interest charges on the loan, don't forget that this cost must be accounted for in the charge you make to your clients.

The **white tablecloths** mentioned above are a very useful asset. Unfortunately, they are very expensive. They also create work because they take a lot of laundering and often need additional soaking, bleaching and starching after a particularly successful and riotous party. Nevertheless, they are invaluable for covering a motley collection of tables or trestles and giving them a look of uniformity, and there is nothing better for setting off colourful, well-presented food and pretty flower arrangements.

Children's Parties

If you are catering for a children's party you may decide to use disposable cups, plates, dishes and cutlery. These do make sense because they avoid the problem of breakages which are not only expensive but also possibly dangerous. You don't want cut fingers dripping blood into your jellies and meringues – they can damage your reputation as well as spoiling the flavour! Very pretty designs of disposable tableware can be obtained from your local Cash and Carry, supermarket or high street stationer. The French make very chic children's ware and this can often be snapped up quite cheaply in Christmas sales, so keep your eyes open, shop around and check carefully on both price and quality before you buy. There are several things to consider before you make your final choice:

* non-sexist designs – balloons, clowns, animals and so on – are better than anything stridently 'boyish' like cowboys and Indians or 'girlish' like baby dolls and flowers because they can be used for any party
* some disposable ware lasts longer than others as it can be washed and re-used at least two or three times. Obviously, this is only worth buying if it doesn't cost two or three times as much as the sort you use once and throw away because as well as the higher price there's the extra labour to be taken into account. It's almost certain that these will have to be washed carefully by hand not machine
* some designs are more hygienic than others. Mugs with a rim around the top will trap germs that won't be budged by simple washing, so they should never be used twice. This is particularly important with children of primary school age when it's almost certain that one of them is sickening for some childish bug which is just waiting to be spread like wildfire throughout the entire neighbourhood – try not to be the one who provides it with the opportunity it's been waiting for

You might also consider investing in one or two plastic table-cloths if you cater for a lot of juvenile functions. These can be very attractive and immensely labour-saving, since the inevitable spills can be dealt with by simply wiping down with a damp cloth, saving you hours of laundering which may never quite get rid of the stains of fruit and fruit juices completely.

So much for the equipment you will need for food preparation and presentation. You also have other vital equipment requirements if your business enterprise is to thrive.

Transport

You will need a car with a very capacious boot, or an estate car, hatchback or van, to get you and all your food and bits and pieces to and from the event for which you are catering. And you will also need to be able to drive it, which means your own clean driving licence. During my research I met many women who relied upon their husbands, friends or family to ferry them to their destination and pick them up at the end of the function. This is not to be recommended for several reasons:

- it deprives the cook of her flexibility and freedom, independence and self-reliance
- it can cause ill will if the 'chauffeur', who may well have happily volunteered his or her services in the first place, suddenly finds the service becomes a chore or disrupts other activities
- in the case of a husband and wife, if he has to drive her or *vice versa* and there are young children at home, part of the profits from the evening's work will go to a baby-sitter

Besides, transport isn't needed just for the event itself. It is also practically essential for marketing, and there's no guarantee that a driver is going to be available during the day when the cook wants to go to the shops. So, if you are planning to take your freelance catering seriously as an integral part of your life and work, and you haven't yet learned to drive, now is the time to start. It will pay dividends in the long run, even if you do have to pay out quite a lot of money for driving lessons in the first place.

Organisation

You will require a certain amount of office-type equipment if you are to be thoroughly business-like. For example, you will need:

* a telephone, so that would-be customers can get in touch with you easily, and so that you can rally support and helpers
* a typewriter, as type-written letters inspire more confidence in your business acumen than hand-written ones. Don't worry if you are not a trained typist; anyone can make a go of two-finger typing with just a little bit of practice, and you will find that your speed and accuracy will gradually improve
* photocopier, if you can afford it. These can often be picked up very cheaply second hand, and a small simple model should be sufficient for your needs when you start up in business. It will certainly work out cheaper than having to make repeated visits to a printer to get documents copied. You should always keep copies, either photostats or carbon copies, of letters, bills, receipts, price quotes, agreements, legal documents and bank statements. These can save hours of argument, and will also make your accounting system much easier
* files for storing your copies, the most useful in my experience being the big box-type ones
* two cash books, one for petty cash and one for the rest of your transactions. These are essential whether you are your own accountant or are able to employ one
* large diary/function book
* wall year-planner chart for recording your engagements
* contact book, containing the names and addresses of all the people, including customers, who can be of use to you
* card-file system of your various menus and recipes
* large filing cabinet, office storage system or capacious desk with several large drawers so that you don't get totally submerged in a sea of paper but can keep every scrap of information neatly tucked away and easily available. It's possible to waste precious hours tracking down an insurance policy, special vegetarian menu or hire purchase agreement

More detailed discussion of the business organisation of your catering enterprise is given in chapter 8.

5
Getting Started and Getting Known

Before you move on to the next stage, it is perhaps sensible to make a checklist of the ground you should already have covered, so that you are absolutely sure you can get off to a flying start. For instance, have you:

* made quite sure in your own mind that you want to be a freelance cook, that you have acquired the relevant skills, not only in cooking but also in organisation and administration, and that you are temperamentally suited to cope with the challenges you will almost certainly face?
* taken advice from the Small Firms Service?
* made contact with the environmental health officer?
* discussed your project with your local bank manager?
* either found yourself an accountant or mastered the rudiments of accountancy yourself?
* been in touch with your local inspector of taxes?
* checked the legal aspects of your business with a solicitor?
* decided whether you are to be a sole trader, or to set up a partnership, a limited company or a co-operative, and worked out its basic pattern of organisation?
* taken advice from an insurance broker?
* investigated your position as far as National Insurance is concerned?
* found a reliable printer?
* given some thought to the most effective means of advertising?
* worked out your overheads, costs and budgeting realistically?
* arranged your kitchen to give the maximum comfort, efficiency and safety, and acquired sufficient basic equipment, including telephone and transport, for any job that you might be required to undertake?

If you can put a healthy row of ticks beside the above list of questions, then you really are ready, at last, to get started and to get known.

Probably your first move should be to find yourself a good, memorable trading name. It's a great temptation to try to be witty or subtle when you're choosing one – but it's also a great mistake. The cleverness, especially if it's of a literary nature, will probably be lost on other people. What you need is something that describes your function quite clearly so that there is no confusion about the service you offer, and is catchy enough to be memorable, so that when a potential customer is wondering who to contact out of a range of possible caterers, it is your name, and not one of your competitors, that first springs to mind. Some examples which might start you thinking along your own lines are: 'Kathie's Kitchen', 'Cooks Galore', 'Country Catering' and 'Rent-a-Cook'. Those I liked especially among the people I interviewed were: 'Flying Saucers', 'Wooden Spoon' and 'Dial-a-Cake', both because they gave some clue to their main function and because they had a musical or rhythmical ring to them. It's wise to avoid anything which might embarrass people when making a telephone enquiry. I, for instance, would fight shy of asking 'Is that "Fluffy's Flambeaux" speaking?'

There is a certain amount of legislation which applies to business names, and you must take pains not to fall foul of it. It was once necessary to register it with the Registry of Business Names. Now, since the Companies Act of 1981, that has all been changed. If you run a business under a name other than your own you are required by law to display prominently: the **business name,** the **owner's name** and the **business address** on any premises from which the business is conducted and on all documents relating to the business, such as letters, orders, invoices, receipts and bills. You must also supply, if requested to do so, these details, in writing, to any person with whom you are doing business. However, if you trade under your own name, either your surname alone, your surname and initials or your surname and Christian names, this rule does not apply. For example, *either* 'Kathie's Kitchen', Katherine Odstock, Wiltshire House, Bramley, Devon, *or* K. Odstock, Caterer, would keep you on the right side of the law.

Unless you are a limited company, you do not have the sole right to the use of a name, even if you thought it up yourself and it seemed particularly appropriate to your personal circumstances. That does not prevent anyone else from using it. This seems very hard and unfair, but it's the law. If you desperately want the sole right to a name you have no option but to form a limited company, and first you must check with the Companies Registration Office, Crown Way, Maindy, Cardiff CF4 3UZ, that no one else is already using the name you want.

Names are very difficult. You'll probably spend hour after hour trying to come up with something good, then eventually the right one will arrive out of the blue – a flash of inspiration. After talking to many freelance cooks, I came to the conclusion that my experience was typical. My plan was to open up a small coffee shop in a village called Downton. We would sell not only fresh, homemade food, either to eat on the premises or to take away, but also local handmade crafts. I wanted to call the business 'Miranda', thinking of the name in its original meaning of 'things to wonder at' as well as one that sounded both pretty and original. My partners would have none of it. To them, Miranda conjured up images of mermaids and was totally inappropriate. After weeks of deliberation, the day eventually dawned when I had to see the printer. I got together with my partners and said 'I must order our cards and letterheads today or we'll not have them in time for the opening. What on earth are we going to call ourselves?' 'Why not "Downton Coffee and Crafts"?' one of them suggested. It was such a simple solution. It described our enterprise exactly, and the alliteration of the two 'Cs' made it sound catchy and attractive. 'That's it,' we all agreed. 'Perfect!' And so, 'Downton Coffee and Crafts' we were christened, and we never regretted it.

Once you have decided upon your name, you can renew contact with the printer of your choice and get to work on your advertising material and stationery, which must be smart, well designed and eye catching, preferably with an instantly recognisable logo which will become your personal trademark. To begin with, it's a good idea to have printed: **business cards, handbills,** which can double as small posters, **headed notepaper** and **book-matches**. Some people also have **car**

stickers printed. If you have a lot of friends prepared to put these in their cars it can be a particularly useful form of advertising since it is mobile and covers an extensive area. What's more, some shopkeepers who say they haven't room to put up a poster for you may be persuaded to fasten a car sticker in their window since it takes less room and is easier to fit in without concealing their own display.

All your advertising should carry the following basic information: your **personal logo**, your **business name**, your own **name, address and telephone number** and the **nature of the service** you provide, described briefly. That should be enough in the first instance; if anyone wants to know more they can get in touch with you and discuss terms and arrangements in greater detail.

Having acquired your advertising material, the next problem is – where to put it? If you do a tour of your nearest towns and villages you will probably discover a great many potential outlets. It's also worth talking to other people who regularly advertise their events and activities – whether it's the local jobbing gardener, the amateur dramatic group or the local theatre or arts centre – and asking their advice about publicity. They probably have a good idea about what works and what is a waste of time, and will enjoy passing on their tales of triumph and tribulation to you. The traumas of publicity have a knack of bringing people together. Don't be afraid of covering the ground and spreading your net wide. Advertising material should saturate the whole area you hope to serve, not just the square mile around your home, and you must have a reasonably large region to draw on if you hope to attract enough customers to keep you busy and in business.

We managed to get our handbills accepted by: **tourist offices** (remember that these are used by local people hoping to find bright ideas for entertaining themselves and their visitors as well as by tourists), **libraries** (both the central city library and small village ones), the **arts centre**, the **Citizens' Advice Bureau, doctors' and dentists' waiting rooms** where, apparently, anything that takes their patients' minds off their problems is welcome, several **post offices, building societies, hairdressers, launderettes** and a great many **shops**. Of the latter, many, especially gift shops and book shops, were perfectly happy to put a little pile of handbills on their counters or to fasten one up in their window or in an indoor poster display. A lot of corner shops and supermarkets, which said they did not provide a free advertising service of this nature, were nevertheless very happy to put up one of our cards in their 'for sale or wanted' section for a minimal charge, and this we gladly agreed to.

A very effective and cheap way of getting your handbills to the public is to ask your newsagent to have them slipped inside the papers they deliver. Normally they will do this for a very small charge, which it is customary for them to pass on to their delivery boys and girls as a tip. Nowadays, however, most towns have at least one free advertising paper which is delivered to every house. If its publisher will accept your handbills, and some to them do, this is the best one to go for. Remember, though, that if you are asking for this sort of co-operation it makes sense to give something in return. An advertising paper will be much more inclined to distribute your handbill if you are prepared to pay for an advertisement in it.

Advertising in the local press usually pays dividends. Our area's free *Avon Advertiser* has three pages of boxed advertisements, grouped together under the heading 'Expert Services'. The services range from van hire to furniture stripping, from painting and decorating to sweat shirt printing, from signwriting to silver replating. Similarly the weekly *Journal* carries a page entitled 'At Your Service' with the sub-heading 'Local firms and businesses with a service to offer you – ring them for an estimate'. These are the pages everyone turns to automatically if they need a professional service; at least one of the boxes will contain details of a freelance caterer. Here are two chosen completely at random.

ALISON CATERING with the personal touch. Delicious home-cooked buffets for very special occasions. With or without waitress service. Phone XXXXXX

RENT-A-COOK, take the hassle out of entertaining. I will shop, prepare and cook for your dinner party, buffet, reception, freezer etc. In your kitchen or mine. Why not give

me a ring on Anywhere XXX and take the first step towards
enjoying your own party?

At present (1983) a typical charge for a boxed advertisement of
this sort, often including logo, is £28 for 8 weekly insertions.

However, what often attracts more attention in the local press
than advertisements are the stories, which tend not only to be
read but also to be discussed by friends and neighbours so that
the information contained is disseminated twice over, first in
print and secondly by word of mouth. If there is something of
particular interest about your catering operation it may well be
that the chief reporter, who is always on the look-out for good
local news, may like to run a little feature about you.

Obviously there's nothing particularly newsworthy about the
fact that our fictitious Ms K. Odstock has just begun a small
business as a freelance caterer, has chosen the name 'Kathie's
Kitchen' and will be specialising in a wide variety of homemade
flans, tarts and quiches. It's very unlikely that that would merit
many column inches, no matter how desperate the chief reporter
was feeling. But if your particular brand of cooking for cash had
some particularly interesting slant, something that made it
different, even unique, then he or she would think it worth while
following up the story. Suppose, for instance, you were a
specialist in Nepalese dishes, having learned your skills from a
Buddhist monk during a journey through the Himalayas – that's
news! Suppose you were one of a group of school-leavers, unable
to find work, who had decided to form your own business rather
than live on social security benefits – that's news! Suppose you
were one of a number of business men or steel-workers, suddenly
made redundant, who had decided to pool your redundancy pay
to start again in an entirely new way – that's news! So, search
your mind for something, anything, that makes you and your
enterprise special, and see if you can catch the interest of your
local paper.

If the local paper thinks it's newsworthy, then probably your
local radio station will as well. Again, it will be avid for news
from the neighbourhood to fill its schedules, and if you can
supply it then you'll be doing the programme, as well as yourself,
a service. You can find the address and telephone number of your

local BBC radio station at the back of the *Radio Times*. Commercial radio stations will probably be in the telephone book. If you have any difficulty ask the Citizens' Advice Bureau or your reference library to find the details for you.

Another extremely useful publication in which to have your name is the Yellow Pages of the telephone directory. It is not cheap to have an entry inserted but I was told by several cooks that their business had doubled its turnover after being listed there. It's obviously an invaluable contact source and should be carefully considered, if you feel able to double your workload.

As well as advertising through the normal channels and getting your name known by means of the local media, a useful method of promoting your service is by word of mouth, personal recommendation or 'the grapevine'. Always carry some of your business cards with you, ready to hand over if you come across a potential customer or useful contact. Ask your friends to do the same on your behalf. Don't be shy about blowing your own trumpet. Some of the most successful people I spoke to admitted to being quite shameless when it came to talking about themselves and their activities, giving parties to promote their business, following up every possible line which might lead to a booking. It's surprising, and just beginning to be more thoroughly understood in our society, exactly how much information, support and assistance is handed on through 'networks', the spreading webs of people who are linked together through acquaintance, friendship, family, work, mutual interests and social activity. So tell everyone you know what you're up to and you'll be quite astonished to discover how far it will get carried.

Once you begin to cater for functions you may well be able to leave small piles of cards or, better still, personalised book-matches, so that guests who are well pleased with what they are eating and the way in which it is presented can carry away one or two of them to keep for future reference. It is a courtesy to check first of all with your client that it is acceptable for you to do a little unobtrusive self-advertising, but few will say no. If they like you and are pleased with your work, most will be glad to be able to help.

Another way of finding customers is to research the area in which you live to find out who regularly uses caterers and for what sort of event, and then contact them directly and tell them what you have to offer and what your scale of charges is. This straightforward approach seems to be extremely effective, though it takes courage to dive in at the deep end in this manner. One cook I met, Felicity, discovered that both the local hospital and the district council regularly organised rather smart buffet lunches and suppers for visiting guests and dignitaries. She made discreet enquiries and found out who was responsible for the arrangements; then she armed herself with sample menus and price lists, plus references and letters of appreciation from satis-fied customers, and went along and bearded them in their offices. By the time she had finished she had charmed trial contracts out of both organisations and assured herself of about ten profitable engagements in the coming year. She's never looked back since.

Another woman, Liz, noticed, purely by chance, that every lunchtime her town was swarming with workers of every kind, business men, solicitors, shop assistants, estate agents, bank clerks, scurrying about with paper bags bearing the names of local bakers and containing, presumably, pies, pasties, cream buns and filled rolls. It occurred to her that most of them would prefer to relax during their lunchbreak instead of rushing around the streets and queueing up for snacks in crowded shops. She instantly conceived the idea of a 'sandwich service'. She worked out a huge and tempting range of sandwich possibilities, varying not only the fillings but also the butter and the sort of bread used, and including many that were very unusual and totally irresistible – such delicacies as rye bread with prawn butter and shellfish, floury baps with tomato butter and ham, pitta bread with kebabs, and bacon and banana in wheatmeal or granary slices. (If you feel that you would like to be creative with sand-wiches, read Carol Bowen's *The Giant Sandwich Book*, published by Hamlyn in paperback. It's crammed with mouth-watering ideas.)

Having considered her product, Liz then did a careful costing of the ingredients, labour and transport, and worked out a realistic price list. This she sent, with a carefully worded letter of introduction and explanation, to every firm or business in the area that was too small to have its own canteen. She offered to provide and deliver a certain number of sandwiches, at a certain price, at a certain time, five days a week, provided she could be given details of the exact order twenty-four hours ahead; in other words, as she delivered one day she would pick up the order for whatever number and variety of sandwiches was required for the next. Having given the manager about two days to consider her suggestion, she then followed up her written information with a personal telephone call or visit. The response was instant and enormous, beyond her wildest imaginings. So much so that she had to enlist a little posse of sandwich makers to share the load, but the business was profitable and successful. Her organisational problems were eased by the fact that most sandwiches freeze extremely well, so she was often able to work ahead and stock up with supplies so that she was never reduced to panic by an unprecedented demand. After a while, as she gained in experience and self-confidence, she expanded the service by adding interesting soups and salads, in lidded thermal containers, to her basic sandwich range. It wasn't just luck, however, that made hers a success story. She succeeded because she:

- recognised a need
- made an intelligent assessment of how to respond to it
- costed her operation correctly
- did her research and made her contacts carefully
- fulfilled her original undertaking to the letter
- maintained her high standards while holding her prices steady by careful marketing

If she'd made an error of judgement in any one of these fundamentals her enterprise could have been doomed to failure, but she used her brain, her imagination and her skill, and pulled it off.

Good publicity of some sort, varied, well considered, wide spread and accurately aimed, is absolutely vital to any successful business venture. It needs to be thought about, worked at and to have money spent on it. It should never be neglected or underestimated.

Nevertheless, the fact remains that every cook I spoke to was absolutely adamant that most of his or her work came through work already done. 'Once you get your first booking,' Felicity told me, 'and you make a success of it, you're home and dry. Often in just a month or two you can stop advertising completely. The ball keeps on rolling. Business builds up and up, so that sometimes it almost becomes too much for you. Everyone's heard of you from someone else, or been to a party you've catered for, and they all insist that you are just what they need. That can be a very tricky stage. Sometimes you find yourself taking on so much extra casual help to get through a spate of bookings that you're almost out of pocket. It might be more profitable to say "No, sorry" to one or two of the engagements and have a smaller workforce to pay. But, of course, when you're just beginning you're afraid to turn anyone down in case they never ask you again. Not that that's likely. If you've got a good service to sell there are always willing buyers, and if it's in short supply the buyers are even more keen because they think it must be very special. But in the early stages you haven't got the confidence to see it that way, so you rush around like mad trying to do everything and half-killing yourself. But it works the other way too. If you do one or two functions badly – if you arrive late, perhaps, or chaotic, or make a mess in someone's kitchen and don't clean up properly, or if the food is boring or badly presented, or if your bill is bigger than you said it would be, or if your manner is offhand and you offend some of the guests – then all the advertising in the world won't make a ha'porth of difference. Your name will be mud. And mud sticks. No one will want you. It's no good saying you had an off-night but usually you're awfully good. All they will remember, and tell their friends, is that on that particular night you were awfully bad and it would be much wiser for them to look for someone more reliable and consistent.'

So the real nub of getting started and getting known is *you* – your own skill, your own organisational efficiency, your own personality and flair. All the rest, the adverts, the contacts and the local paper coverage, are secondary. Never let them become more important than doing the job well and giving good value, in every sense of the word, for money.

6
Catering Outlets

When you first hit upon the idea of cooking for cash you probably have few preconceived notions of what you are going to cook or who you are going to cook for. You begin with the simple premise that you have a particular skill that you enjoy using, and that other people need and are prepared to pay for. But if you are going to be successful you need to know much more than that. For instance:

- who needs the services of a freelance cook?
- what form of catering do they need?
- who else in your neighbourhood is providing a catering service?
- what sort of service, what standards and what charges do they set for it?

The market will also depend upon:

- where you live
- what help is available
- what cooking skills you possess
- what cooking skills you most enjoy using

If you are based in a large town or city which has a population of reasonably affluent, sociable and busy people, the world's your oyster and you can find whichever pearl you prefer. In a country area opportunities are obviously much more limited, and may revolve more around village weddings and football club dances than smart dinner parties and elegant buffet suppers. Similarly, if you are Cordon Bleu trained, with a flair for pâté de canard lucullus and pork noisettes with prunes in cream sauce, you'll not necessarily be at your best providing bangers and mash for the local Darby and Joan Club or hamburgers and coke for a teenage disco. If you feel more at your ease providing gourmet food for half a dozen civilised adults, you may loathe organising a noisy, distinctly uncivilised children's tea party. If you enjoy cooking good, simple, English food – and it's difficult to find anything more perfect of its kind than a really well-made steak and kidney pie or beef and Yorkshire pudding – you'll perhaps not enjoy grappling with the complexities of tournedos with white wine or escalopes de veau cauchoise.

All of these limitations and restrictions need careful considera-tion. You must also consider your own motivation. If your main aim is to develop an enjoyable hobby and make a little pocket money or extra housekeeping cash on the side, then you can afford to pick and choose and have fun. If, however, you really need to earn extra income, then it's wise to become a jack of all trades, take on as much work as is viable without running up a huge wages bill, master as many cooking skills as possible and find helpers with complementary skills to lend a hand with any engagements that may seem a bit beyond you.

It's also a good idea to have a special expertise that isn't generally available. For example, many people now are calorie conscious and would enjoy a meal more if they didn't think it was going to pile on the pounds. So, a special and delicious series of slimmers' menus might be a useful card to have up your sleeve. The bookshops are brimming over with books about cookery for slimmers, but you could make a start with *The Low Calorie Menu Book* by Joyce Hughes and Audrey Eyton, published by *Slimming Magazine*, as well as picking up a copy of the magazine occasionally. It's usually packed with excellent menus and recipes, with lots of general food and cookery tips.

And there's a growing interest in vegetarianism and wholefood cookery. You could easily make yourself an expert in this area. Two splendid books that made me realise how appetising health foods could be were the *Whole Earth Cookbook* by Sharon Cadwallader and Judi Ohr, published by Penguin, and *Not Just a Load of Old Lentils* by Rose Elliot, published by Fontana. But these are just the tip of a very large iceberg.

This strange combination of versatility plus special expertise is the mark of a thoroughly professional freelance, and it applies to all types of work. Whether you are an interior decorator, a

builder, a self-employed hairdresser, a musician, an actress or
journalist, if you are making a career for yourself you are bound
to find that at some time or another you are doing work you may
not feel totally happy about, or well-qualified or suited for. The
answer, as I have found from experience, is not to reject it, but to
accept it, prepare for it thoroughly, master its problems and then
do as good a job as you possibly can. That is the hallmark of the
professional. It's up to you whether you choose to be an amateur
or a professional, but if you decide to be the latter you have to
come up with the goods, how, when and where required. This is
not as depressing as it may sound, for three very good reasons.
The first is that any job can bring with it enormous satisfaction,
pride and self-assurance if you know you have done it well. The
second is that if you begin in this way you may well build up
such a reputation that you will eventually reach the stage where
you can pick and choose. The third is that if you try your hand at
anything, it's possible that you will find that you are very good
at, and enjoy, doing things which may have seemed totally
unappealing. I have often found that I have gained great excitement and pleasure from commissions which I could well have
turned down if I had not needed to be busy and earning.

Having talked to hundreds of freelance cooks during the course
of a year, I have gathered together a list of the many types of
catering outlets which they have discovered or developed for
themselves. Some are very obvious, and it's a comparatively easy
matter to find them and get involved in them. Others are much
more specialised. Some of them are possible wherever you live.
Others, like preparing Glyndebourne picnic hampers or freezer
filling for holiday cottages, are only possible in certain parts of
the country. Some can be done on a shoestring, with minimal
capital, space, cooking facilities and equipment. Others, like
opening a shop or operating from a van, need an influx of money,
the nerve to take a risk with your savings and the determination
to grapple with red tape. Some can be done single-handed.
Others depend upon group activity. Some may seem boring.
Others can be enormous fun. Some, like making cakes for someone else's shop or café, can be very lonely. Others, like running a
co-operative restaurant in an arts centre or theatre, are very
sociable activities. But all are possible.

In chapter 10 you will find interviews with fifteen people involved in one or more of these projects; their reaction to the pleasures and problems of their work should give you a clearer idea of what sort of area you would most enjoy operating in, provided that you live in the right sort of place and are able to organise a similar type of project. The list does not pretend to be complete or definitive. You will, without doubt, be able to find many more possibilities of your own to add or develop a wide range of variations on a given theme. But it should contain sufficient ideas to start you thinking along the right lines and fire your imagination in one direction or another.

Community Catering

First of all, let's begin with what I would call, for simplicity's sake, community catering, that is, providing meals for organisations or groups. This can include low-budget, unsophisticated, but well-cooked and attractively presented parties, teas, suppers or lunches for societies like **sports clubs, old people's clubs, church or chapel groups** and **village associations**, such as the horticultural society, the local history group, the amateur dramatic association and so on. Alternatively, you could provide rather more specialised refreshments for **youth club celebrations**, which may take the form of a disco, barbecue, beach party or picnic, or **children's parties**, organised by a church, school or club, either indoors or outdoors, according to the time of year and the weather. Two things to remember with children and teenagers is that for the most part they have not yet developed a palate for fine food, and that they frequently prefer savoury dishes to sweet things. My personal experience has been that sausages, hamburgers, pies, pasties, pizzas, hot dogs, chicken joints, crisps, crisps and more crisps – all the things we tend to write off as 'junk food' – are 'in', and more wholesome and nutritious meat dishes or traditional children's sweets, like jelly and trifle, are 'out', though few of them can resist ice-cream, especially flavoured ice-cream, with chocolate coming top of the list.

A rather up-market version of community catering is organising **civic or official functions and receptions.** These can range from small luncheon buffets for a dozen or so to massive dinners or dinner dances for two to three hundred or more. Needless to say, the latter should not be taken on lightly. Unless you are absolutely sure that you have access to the vast amount of equipment, extra labour and temporary storage you will need, can get your costings right and are sufficiently well organised to mastermind such a venture, it is better not to accept the booking. If you do it and do it badly, your reputation might never recover. On the other hand, if you do it and do it well, then it will be worth a great deal to you in valuable publicity. You need to be realistic about your limitations, but once you have decided that a job, however large, is within your limitations, you must make sure that you do it excellently.

Very often civic and official catering engagements go to those who are known in some way. A personal recommendation is much more likely to be followed up than an advertisement, so it is useful if you have contacts within the organisation, whether it is the district council, a political party or whatever. If you don't know anyone you can approach personally, there's absolutely no reason why you shouldn't write to the person responsible for social functions, sending him or her a copy of your sample menus and price lists, and copies of a few letters of recommendation and appreciation, and suggest that you should meet and discuss possibilities. (Always include a stamped addressed envelope or you'll be lucky to receive a reply.) It's not always easy to know who to address your letter to, but often a few discreet enquiries in the right quarters will give you a lead. If it's the district council you're interested in, write to the chairman's personal secretary who will direct correspondence to the appropriate recipient. The business of introducing yourself and your service, of doing a little stylish self-advertising, should be an integral part of your work when you are setting up as a caterer, though after a while it shouldn't be necessary. At worst, you can be ignored or your offer rejected. Possibly you will be told that there's nothing to offer you at the moment, but your details will be kept on file for future reference. If so, follow it up at regular intervals, but not too regular or they will think you are wasting their time. At best, you may open up a very profitable avenue of regular work and an extensive network of valuable contacts.

Business or Industrial Catering

Very similar to official and civic catering is the world of business catering. Again, it tends to be formal, and therefore it needs to be carefully structured and organised. At a rollicking family party a small error of timing or presentation is hardly likely even to be noticed, let alone criticised, but these things matter mightily when money is the main motivation.

Again, the route in to business entertaining is usually through who you know or who knows you, but there's no need to leave it entirely to chance. There's no law against a little gentle manipulation. You should find it quite easy, just by asking around, to discover which firms need occasional caterers. Some of them, of course, have their own catering departments. In a small community at any rate, it should not be difficult to make contact with someone who could introduce you, or at least your name, to a useful contact.

Business catering takes many forms, one of them being the regular sandwich/soup/salad service described in the previous chapter. There are also occasional special requirements which may fit in better with your organisation, and these are worth knowing about. It may be that a short-list of applicants is being interviewed for a job and that the preliminary to the interviews is a buffet lunch where members of the interviewing panel can talk informally to the candidates. It may be that a farewell party has been arranged for a retiring employee or that a reception is being held to mark the inauguration of a special advertising drive, a sponsorship project or the anniversary of the firm's foundation. Or it may be that the firm is having a public relations stand at a trade fair or agricultural show where potential customers are given refreshments in order to boost their enthusiasm. A caterer will be needed for all these events.

Social Catering

The next set of possibilities to consider can be loosely grouped together as social catering, that is, the organising of social events for private individuals who are celebrating in some way, or simply entertaining friends or family. The variety of these occasions is enormous, and can range from roisterous, low-budget wedding parties in the village hall to urbane suppers for six in a sophisticated pied-à-terre, from noisy teenage discos to sedate Golden Weddings, from exuberant children's birthdays to solemn and subdued funeral receptions. It is up to you, your temperament, your talent and your financial situation to decide which of these bookings you might like to take on, given the opportunity. Unless you are extremely versatile, adaptable and temperamentally equable, it's unlikely that you would get the same amount of satisfaction from them all, or that you would be equally adept at coping with them all.

But don't shy away from possibilities just because the idea is new to you. There are always good, instructive, helpful books available, either from your library or in paperback from your bookseller, to give you all the information you need to get started and, once you've done it the first time and made a success of it, you'll never have to face the same nagging self-doubts again. If, however, you make a mess of it the first time, it's a different kettle of fish. You'll then have to decide whether you are just not cut out for that particular type of catering and have no desire to repeat the uncomfortable experiment or that you made mistakes but learned by them, so that if you get a second chance you will know how to make a success of it. The following books should give you confidence and sufficient sound advice to cope with specialised engagements that you have not yet mastered: *Barbecues* by James F. Marks, published by Penguin; *Picnic* by Claudia Roden, published by Penguin; *Party Cooking* edited by Jean Prince, published by Octopus; *The Good Food Guide's Dinner Party Books* by Hilary Fawcett, published by the Consumers' Association; *The Entertaining Cookbook* by Evelyn Rose, published by Fontana.

You could even initiate your own form of social catering, and move into an area that has as yet hardly been touched. Remembering the value of being newsworthy which we discussed in chapter 5, it is obvious that the business of running a completely new, original or unique type of service cannot help but hit the headlines. The 'Dial-a-Cake' idea which Tim Charlton describes in his interview in chapter 10 has hardly been tapped in this country and offers limitless possibilities to anyone with the energy and initiative to launch such an enterprise. Another untapped source is the great British breakfast.

When I was at university it was the custom for the smartest and most sophisticated of the students to celebrate their twenty-first birthdays with festive breakfasts, and yet breakfast or brunch catering has still not got off the ground. It is comparatively uncharted country for those with the pioneering spirit and has much to commend it, especially during the summer months when the early part of the day is often the most beautiful, and it may be possible to serve it in the garden. An up-market, Cordon Bleu, home-delivered breakfast service could be an enterprising way of extending a freelance catering operation, especially since it uses up those hours which are left free by evening engagements, and can therefore double productivity.

The breakfast need not necessarily be a large party. For instance, you could do a luxurious breakfast-in-bed service as a surprise anniversary gift for the couple who has everything. It would be a splendid way to begin a Silver Wedding, with a touch of the second honeymoon. Imagine freshly squeezed fruit juice, smoked bacon, grilled kidneys and field mushrooms, newly baked croissants with unsalted butter and homemade marmalade, ground coffee and cream – perhaps Bucks Fizz or champagne too! – all served on silver trays, with silver-edged napkins and a single red rose in a silver vase. That sort of treat will still be fragrant in the memory of the happy couple when they have reached their Golden Wedding day and are clamouring for a return booking!

The idea could be extended. A welcome-home gift for friends or relatives returning after a long absence, a present for happy lovers, even a birthday surprise for a child or young teenager, preferably with other youngsters staying overnight in the house so that they can share in the fun. Once the idea caught on I'm sure it would grow. It could even be the cult of the future since an opulent and extravagant breakfast, especially in bed, manages to seem slightly decadent while being perfectly respectable, and that's an irresistible combination. For more information and ideas about imaginative and creative breakfasts have a look at *The Breakfast Book* by David St John Thomas, published by David & Charles.

Commercial Catering

Another area for the freelance cook to explore can be described as commercial rather than social, since it is much more to do with the business side of food supply than the entertainment side.

Retail Outlet Cooking

Many cake shops, pubs, delicatessen and cafés rely heavily on home-based cooks to provide them with their stock, whether the demand is for chocolate gateaux, quiches, pâtés or steak and mushroom puddings. This type of catering has much to commend it. For instance, if you have a flair for making short-bread and brandy snaps and have an order for two or three tins of each every week, month in, month out, come what may, you can fulfil your commitment very easily and be assured of a regular income. You can do the work when you want, fitting it in easily between other activities as best suits you. If you are busy one week, ill or on holiday, it is a simple matter to do twice your order another week and always maintain a reserve supply. You don't need to worry about publicity or advertising, and you know you have a steady market, with no risk and no wastage.

But there are disadvantages too. Often the going rate of pay is only twice the cost of the ingredients plus a small reimbursement for gas or electricity used, so you may be receiving a very small financial return for long hours spent in the kitchen. If you are cooking the same one or two items regularly, with little variety and no scope for imagination or creativity, the work can become excessively boring. And since your only personal contact is likely to be with the retail outlet and not with the public, there is little social satisfaction since you miss out on the real pleasure of seeing people eat and enjoy the fruits of your labours. In other words, you may experience many of the irritations that home-based workers in any manufacturing industry complain of – especially poor pay and lack of job satisfaction. So you would be wise to consider the pros and cons very carefully before you get too deeply involved in this form of work. If you really need the money, however little it is, if you have to be at home most of the time and if you thoroughly enjoy both the cooking and the feeling that you are doing something useful, that's fine. But if not, this sort of cooking for cash is probably better regarded as a fill-in, augmenting other kinds of catering, rather than as a sole occupation.

Freezer Cooking

Freezer cooking is becoming something of a growth industry. The idea is simply to fill up someone's deep freeze with a wide variety of homemade dishes – perhaps a month's supply of things like cakes, puddings, pies, flans, casseroles and soups – thus relieving them of the double chore of shopping and cooking/baking. Sometimes the customers are busy professional people who have neither the time nor the inclination to cook for themselves but don't want to exist on shop-bought convenience foods. Sometimes they are people who do a lot of entertaining and prefer to pay for the privilege of being able to take gourmet dishes out of their own deep freeze rather than attempt to do the cooking themselves or employ a caterer of the more traditional school. Very often they are old or incapacitated people, who simply are not able to do their own cooking, and sometimes their family or friends organise the filling of their freezer to give them a modicum of independence.

Some freezer cooks do the work in the client's kitchen, using the power, equipment and ingredients supplied, and charge only for their time and labour. Others provide their own ingredients, cook in their own kitchens and then deliver a certain number of dishes, usually in disposable foil containers to eliminate either washing up or subsequent collection of crockery, having agreed a specific price for each item beforehand. Almost all have a preliminary discussion with the client to draw up a list of what is required, and this is probably a compromise between what the customer asks for and what specialities the cook can offer.

The range of freezer food is vast. There's hardly anything that can't be frozen in some form or other. Consequently, it has to be whittled down to personal preferences and practicalities, and it makes sense to avoid anything that takes hours and hours of preparation unless you can get a very good price for it. It's also very important to get the size of the dish right. If you are cooking for an elderly couple with sparrow appetites you may make five pounds of steak and kidney casserole, but it must be packed into small containers holding only two portions each, otherwise they will eat nothing but steak and kidney casserole for a week and still have to throw some of it away at the end. If you are preparing for a party, larger containers can, of course, be safely used, but as a general rule it is better to freeze food in small portions, allowing customers to heat up several at the same time if need be, rather than in over-generous ones which may go to waste.

Freezer cooking can be quite satisfying, especially if the cooking is done in the customer's kitchen, perhaps with a partner, since it gets you out and about, enables you to meet a lot of people and presents you with both culinary and practical challenges. But always have a very careful look at the kitchen and its equipment before you arrive to do the cooking. There's almost certain to be something missing, or complicated, that you need to take account of beforehand. On one horrifying occasion I found myself faced with a tin opener – absolutely vital for my can of tomato purée – which was so like a Heath Robinson invention that I couldn't begin to work out how to use it. Since my customer had taken herself off for the day leaving me entirely to my own devices, and an exhaustive search of her kitchen failed to reveal an alternative tin opener for the simple-minded, I had no alternative but to waste precious time and petrol in a three-mile dash back to my own kitchen. If you are tied to your own kitchen and can't do the cooking on other people's premises, freezer cookery might be a rather lonely occupation, but can still give the keen cook the satisfaction of making a wide variety of dishes, making them well and being confident that her skills will bring pleasure; in some cases she will also know that she is providing a valuable social service.

If your food is enjoyed the first time, the bookings are likely to become regular and more numerous as time goes by, and will bring in an assured income all year round with extra bonuses as Christmas and party time draws near. However, the chances are it will not be a very large income. One freezer cook, who worked with a partner, told me, 'When we calculated the hours we spent, we realised we were being very badly underpaid for our skills. It wasn't that we had got our costings wrong. It's not as simple as that. The truth is that some of the supermarkets now sell extremely good frozen food – delicious fish pies and cream gateaux, all sorts of luxury items. And though people are prepared to pay a certain amount extra for the special flavour of home-cooking and individual recipes, there is a limit. Most of them wouldn't pay twice as much, for example, though they might pay half as much again. So we had to watch the prices of Bejam, Sainsburys, Safeways, Marks and Spencer, all the big names, and make sure that we didn't price ourselves out of the market. Consequently we never really felt we were earning what we could earn in other forms of catering. There wasn't the stress of putting on a party, less rushing around, less worry – but less profit too.' It's a point worth considering. Many cooks begin with freezer cooking but then move on to other things.

Holiday Home Freezer Cookery

Another form of freezer cooking has begun to flourish quite recently in holiday areas where there are a large number of self-catering flats and cottages to let. As an optional extra amenity, the owner or agent of the holiday home can arrange to have a deep freeze filled with sufficient food to keep the holiday-makers well fed with minimal effort on their part throughout their stay. This will obviously cost them more than doing their own cater-ing from scratch but much less than eating out in cafés, hotels and restaurants every night, so for many it's a very attractive proposition. Usually a list of available dishes, plus prices, is sent to them as soon as the booking is confirmed and they are able to select and send in their order two or three weeks before arrival. Again, this is a safe freelance option because it is only necessary to provide what you know is required, so there are no financial risks, nor is there the expense of advertising. But it is not a big money-spinner, for several reasons. First, the agency or individual letting the holiday homes is likely to insist on charging you a commission on sales in return for providing you with customers. Secondly, the customers themselves might not feel that there's enough cash in their holiday kitty to splash out on a service of this nature and prefer to exist on bangers and beans or fish and chips, so some weeks there might be little call for your cooking. The greatest disadvantage, however, is the seasonal aspect of this type of business. There may be several long lean months when the holiday homes stand empty, their freezers unfilled, and the busiest time will certainly clash with your own need for a holiday or the time when your own family commitments are heaviest.

This is the sort of business venture that depends upon many factors which you need to consider before you get involved, so ask yourself the following questions:

- do I live in an area which attracts comparatively affluent, self-catering holiday-makers?
- can I persuade holiday home owners or agents that it is in their interest to co-operate with me and send out my information material to their prospective customers?
- am I able and happy to work hard during the holiday period and have time on my hands for the rest of the year?
- can I tie in this particular type of catering with some other venture in order to ensure continuity of both work and income?
- am I sure that I am completely reliable and have foolproof back-up in case I have some crisis and cannot fulfil my commitment? (If a disappointed holiday-maker complains that you have let him down and not produced what you promised to deliver you will have spoilt his holiday and your own reputation)

Freezer Food Take-away

Holiday home freezer cookery may tie in very well with a freezer food take-away business based in your own home. This is quite easy to organise provided that both the environmental health officer and the planning department are quite happy that you aren't infringing any of their regulations. All you need do is fill your freezer with an appetising range of gourmet dishes, advertise your wares, distribute your price list, try to persuade customers to order what they want beforehand – while at the same time remaining flexible enough to provide food for those who suddenly find themselves confronted by unexpected visitors, an empty larder or a sudden, undeniable craving for profiteroles! – and keep your freezer well stocked.

This sort of business flourishes when it can provide genuinely up-market quality dishes that most people wouldn't or couldn't make themselves, but would enjoy offering to their friends at parties and celebrations. For instance, the menu list could include such delicacies as bortsch, vichyssoise, crab bisque, salmon mousse, cassoulet and navarin of lamb printanier, sorbets, crème brûlée and charlotte malakoff. There is a positive plethora of books available which deal with freezing techniques and recipes, but the one I turn to again and again is the excellent *Penguin Freezer Cookbook* by Helge Rubinstein and Sheila Bush. I also use *Growing, Freezing and Cooking* by Mary Norwak and Keith Mossman, and *Deep Freezing Menus and Recipes* by Mary Norwak, both published by Sphere.

I do find that cookery books are like people. Some you take to naturally and they become your friends for life; others you never really feel at home with, though you may never be able to work out why. Consequently, my own favourites may not appeal to you at all. The only thing I can do is mention them in passing and allow you to take them or leave them, according to your inclination.

Food Hampers

Another way of balancing a seasonal business like holiday catering is to make up food hampers, especially at Christmas. These make excellent presents, especially for the elderly or for those lucky folks who seem to have everything but still need to eat. If they are packed with superb homemade delicacies, they are especially acceptable. They are also great fun to prepare. The imagination can run riot as far as the contents are concerned. As well as basics like cake, pudding and biscuits, they can contain delicious sweets – turkish delight, coconut ice and flavoured fudge perhaps. And there can be honey and jams, pickles and preserves, herb vinegars and teas. (Do make sure, though, that everything is properly labelled, showing where it comes from, what it weighs, the main ingredients and the name of the producer, otherwise you could fall foul of the law. If in doubt, talk to the environmental health officer and the Weights and Measures Department before you get going, just to be on the safe side.)

It's a good idea to make up a list of possible contents for the hamper and allow customers to choose their own selection of goodies. This also means that you can have three or four separate prices, depending on the value and number of the items chosen for inclusion. Everything must, of course, be presented beautifully. With this sort of gift packaging is half the pleasure.

How you actually set about selling your hampers also needs thought. If there's an effective 'grapevine' in your community, it's possible that word of mouth will do your advertising for you and friends and acquaintances will approach you directly with their orders. Or you can put an advertisement in nearby shops or the local paper. It's tempting, but not, I think, a good idea, to get involved in mail order. Not only is this formidably expensive, but effective protective wrapping is very difficult and there's always the possibility of breakages. Delivery delays can occur too and, though they may be no fault of your own, they can be very damaging to your reputation. It's absolutely infuriating to order what seems like the perfect present only to have it arrive days late or smashed to pieces.

Probably one of the best ways of selling is through a local craft shop or delicatessen. They may be persuaded to display a demonstration hamper, plus your list of possible contents and prices, and take orders for you. But they will, of course, charge you commission, perhaps only 10 per cent since it involves no financial risk for them and can be an added attraction for their customers.

Cake Making and Decorating

Many caterers make money through their expertise in anniversary cake making and/or decorating. Special cakes are in demand all year round for birthdays, weddings and anniversaries of all kinds. This can be a very creative job since the skill lies not so much in baking the cake – though that, of course, has to taste good – but more in the decoration. Cake decoration is almost an art form in itself, ranging from the traditional wedding cake, with its lovers' knots, hearts and roses of icing, to children's cakes which can take the form of trains, cars, boats, space ships, dolls' houses, football stadiums – whatever reflects the interests of the lucky child.

Betty, a retired school meals supervisor, told me that she found it a totally absorbing occupation. 'I get completely carried away,' she said. 'Once I start the icing process I lose all track of time. I have a picture in my head, sometimes roughed out on paper too, and I put my whole concentration into creating that picture in three-dimensional terms. Far from being lonely when I'm closeted in the kitchen with my icing and colouring and piping equipment and decorations, I really resent being interrupted. I just want to go on and on until it's finished. There's enormous satisfaction in it. First the pleasure of seeing that the finished product looks good. Then, very often, the pleasure of going along to the party and seeing for myself how much my work is appreciated. That moment when the knife goes in and I see that the inside of the cake looks just as appetising as the decorative outside takes some beating. I never have to tout for business, the orders come flooding in, so many of them sometimes that I have to refuse one or two. But it's not a money-spinner. I suppose I double the cost of the ingredients when I fix a final price. A grand wedding cake, three or four tiers, might fetch as much as £60 or £70, and half of that is profit. But the hours of work involved, and the shopping, and the cost of electricity, give quite a low hourly return for the work put in. I only do it because I love doing it. Other retired people get their pleasure from painting, or playing golf – I get mine from icing cakes.'

If this is the sort of thing you would like to do, but don't know how to start, make enquiries at your local library. It's usually possible to enrol for a cake decoration class somewhere in your locality, especially in the autumn; often there are one-day demonstrations too, maybe at your nearest Women's Institute or Townswomen's Guild. The best book I've come across so far on the subject is *Cake Decorating and Sugarcraft* by Evelyn Wallace, published by Hamlyn, which covers much the same ground as a course of classes would do. However, it is probably better to receive your instruction in person rather than in print, and then use the book as a reminder of what you have learned and to extend your ideas and imagination.

Markets

Markets are useful places in which a freelance cook can sell his or her wares. Most of them are very busy, and many shoppers are on the prowl for good quality, reasonably priced goods that they can't buy in the shops. At least, they probably can't buy them at the same price in the shops because market stallholders don't have the high overheads that shopkeepers are burdened with. Consequently, they can command a reasonable profit margin while still keeping their prices low.

The market that impressed me most during my research was the Women's Institute Co-operative Market, a sales outlet that is formidably well organised, thoroughly efficient and maintains impeccably high standards of quality, flavour and hygiene. It is not necessary to be a member of the Women's Institute, or even a woman, to sell through their market, merely a shareholder in their local Market Society, and for this privilege you pay the princely sum of 5p for life membership. The WI market organisation has an interesting history. It was started after World War I, in a time of economic depression and social unrest not unlike our own, to help not only WI members but also unemployed men, retired ex-servicemen and old age pensioners to sell the surplus produce from their gardens and kitchens, and thus give a small boost to their income. Now, more than half a century later, much has changed, but basically the aims are the same:

* to make it financially worth while to keep gardens in cultivation
* to help an increasing number of people to develop their skills and see them as a financial asset, whether their expertise lies in gardening, cooking, or craftwork
* to do this by working together co-operatively

During our present period of recession, with its high unemployment figures, the market is coming to the aid of people's self-respect and dignity, and giving them some motivation, in exactly the same way as it did fifty years ago. One controller told me an interesting story about a young boy who lived in her village: 'David had left school and was quite unable to get a job. For months and months he hung around the house and didn't seem to be interested in anything. The only thing he enjoyed was helping his father in their garden and allotment, and gradually he took over more and more of the work and grew some excellent vegetables. One day he wandered into the market to buy something for his mother, and saw our stalls of garden produce. Next week his mother came and said "David would love to get involved in something like this – what a shame it's just for WI members!" We rapidly assured her that that was not the case, and David would be very welcome to sell through us, provided that his produce was good enough, and properly packed and presented. Well, he took to it like a duck to water, brought us wonderful things week after week, unusual vegetables, herbs and plants, all top quality. Often he stayed to serve too. One of his specialities was lovely little Victorian posies of flowers – so pretty and unusual – all done up in doilies and ribbons. That led to him being asked to do bouquets for weddings, and flower arrangements for parties and dances and concerts in the village, as well as extending his allotment work. He made a little bit of money, but that wasn't the important thing. He was busy, very busy. He had commitments. And everyone was so impressed with his skills and his business-like approach that it was a marvellous boost to his confidence. He really was a changed boy. The story had a happy ending because after three months or so he got a job. No, not in gardening, as it happened, but on a local farm. He still occasionally sends us odds and ends to sell for him but I think other interests are beginning to take over. That doesn't matter though – we helped him through a sticky patch, and he helped us, and that's what it's all about.'

As well as crafts and garden produce, eggs, poultry and rabbit, the WI markets sell: **preserves, fruit syrups, cakes, bread, savouries, sweets** and **dairy produce,** but not homemade wines or yoghurts. No produce is sold unless it is absolutely fresh and of good quality, and it must conform to the requirements of three separate bits of legislation:

- the Weights and Measures Act (the customer must be informed of weight and measure, and scales must be kept at hand for a check to be made if necessary)
- the Trades Description Act (for example, if the label states 'butter icing' the icing must have been made from butter and not from margarine)
- the Food Hygiene Regulations (these cover the protection of food from contamination, the wearing of protective aprons,

personal cleanliness on the part of cooks and servers, adequate supplies of hot water, soap, towels and nail brushes both where the food is prepared and at the market, clean utensils and working surfaces)

The market also has its own rigidly enforced standards. For example:

* nothing sold there, whether cooked or uncooked, must have been taken out of a freezer
* everything must conform to the stringent rules laid down about packaging and presentation
* labelling must be very precise

Two very helpful booklets, *The WI Market Handbook* and *Markets, Pleasure and Profit*, both published by The National Federation of Women's Institutes, 39 Eccleston Street, London, SW1W 9NT are useful, readable and give much more detailed information than space allows here.

It may seem to you that all this care and maintenance of high standards is not worth the trouble entailed, especially since this most certainly is not a way to make a lot of money. The following guideline is laid down to enable cooks to arrive at a fair price for cooked or preserved produce that will give a reasonable return for labour. Add together the cost of all ingredients and equipment used, ie ingredients, plus jars, bottles, jam pot lids, labels, foil plates, cake bags etc. To this sum add one-third of the total to cover the cost of time and fuel, and to this total add one-half, as profit, for example:

Ingredients plus equipment	90p
Plus one-third for time and fuel	30p
	£1.20p
Plus one-half for profit	£1.80p

In other words, double it! That extra 90p, however, is not all yours because you have to pay the market a commission to cover the cost of organisation, which is right and proper since it has provided you with a desirable sales outlet and ready-made customers. The amount of commission deducted is decided by the shareholders themselves at their annual meeting where they will be advised by the treasurer and committee, who have observed and regulated the finances of the market during the year and are best able to judge the financial health of the organisation. Normally the commission ranges between 10 and 15 per cent according to the cost of overheads such as rent, rates and equipment. So, you may lose between 18p and 27p of the £1.80 you received – and remember only part of that was profit.

I discovered that most people who sell through the WI are very happy to do so, and revel in their participation in this huge, nationwide organisation which now has over 450 markets and an annual turnover approaching £4,000,000. Their pleasure derives from several different sources. For example, though no one earns a great deal, it is possible to sell through several different markets and therefore multiply your takings until you make quite a reasonable sum. The money earned is nearly always salted away for a specific purpose, for some object which might otherwise be impossible, and this invests it with a sense of achievement. For instance, Jenny told me, 'I have a very musical daughter who plays two different instruments and therefore has to have two music lessons a week. Not cheap these days – but my cakes pay for them!' Pat was helping to pay off a hefty mortgage. If it hadn't been for her earnings she and her husband wouldn't have been able to buy the house of their choice. 'I cheat a bit, I suppose,' she confessed. 'I pay for the actual ingredients out of my housekeeping, then put all my takings into the building society. It's surprising what a difference it makes, even if it's just £40 or £50 a month.' With Sheila, the cooking paid for her car. 'It's just a little old banger. I bought it for a song. But I earn enough to keep it on the road, tax, insurance and petrol, so it gives me mobility and independence. My husband, bless his heart, pays for all the maintenance and servicing – he says it's worth it to stop me moaning about being stuck in the house without my own set of wheels.'

But the satisfaction goes much deeper than mere financial reward. These are all women who love to cook. Betty made superb brown bread, twenty large loaves a week. 'I love baking bread. It's therapeutic, all that kneading,' she laughed. 'I do it in the kitchen, after tea, with all the children round me, talking, giggling, telling me about their day at school, and it's really fun. Part of family life. Much better than sitting in hushed silence watching the telly! The other nice thing is that people enjoy eating my bread so much that I always have a load of orders, and that's very good for the ego.' Ethel was elderly, living alone, her children having long since left home. 'Cooking's about the only thing I'm good at,' she told me. 'Steak and kidney pies and puddings, beef casseroles, apple tarts, plain English cooking. But now I've got no one to cook for, so this seemed the answer. I bring it down here and it sells in a flash, and gives me a little extra for the odd luxury. I'm saving up for a holiday to see my grandchildren soon.'

There is also patent pride in the feeling of having accepted the challenge of very high standards of both cooking and packaging, and having proved that you can meet them. Nothing goes on sale on a WI market stall until it has got past the rigorous eye of the controller. Only if she is totally satisfied that it is up to standard, is it accepted. If she decides it is not up to standard, then the product is rejected, but the cook is told why it has been turned down, given an explanation and some pointers as to how she can improve her work, and encouraged to try again. Consequently, everyone who is selling has already been awarded a mark of excellence. Those who are selling and receiving orders for next week, or sometimes even standing orders for weeks in advance, have yet more cause for pleasure and enjoy a comfortable boost to their self-esteem.

The primary satisfaction, however, seems to stem from the social element of the market – the feeling of companionship that the cooks share, the pleasure of serving on the stalls and seeing their work praised, the relationship with their customers, many of whom are regulars, and the fact that market day gives a focal point to their week. Jane is nearly eighty, but active and sprightly. Recently widowed, she admits to being lonely and planning her time carefully to avoid boredom. 'I always look forward to our market day,' she says. 'On Wednesday I think what I'm going to make, and do any shopping that's necessary. Thursday is baking day. Friday morning is market day and I sometimes serve on one of the stalls. Sometimes I just bring my food down and have a cup of coffee and a nice little social get-together with the others. Sometimes I find lovely plants on the garden produce stalls – I'm a very keen gardener still – and I can buy fresh fruit and vegetables here if I need them. It's a high spot of the week. Something to give it shape. And that's important when you're on your own. If there's no shape, no routine, time seems to drag on and on.'

It's not only the WI that has its markets, of course. There are markets still flourishing in market towns throughout the country, as well as in many parts of London and other big cities, and there is nothing to stop you, either alone but preferably with a group of friends, hiring a stall in one of them and selling your wares from it – provided, that is, you can get a stall as there's often a waiting list. First of all make contact with the market superintendent and discuss your plan with him. He's almost certain to have an office very near the market and any of the stall-holders will be able to direct you to it. You must also be very careful to obey the legal requirements of the three articles of legislation already mentioned with reference to the WI market organisation. You will be able to study the Trades Description Act and the Weights and Measures Act at any reasonably sized library where you will probably find them in the reference department, although it's perhaps a better idea to go to your local Citizens' Advice Bureau first of all. They won't simply hand you two incomprehensible tomes of bureaucratic language and expect you to wade through them alone; they'll take the time and trouble to sit down with you and discuss the problem.

To find out more about the relevant food hygiene regulations drop in at the office of your local district council and ask to see the environmental health officer. In my experience these people are very helpful, positive, constructive and knowledgeable when it comes to giving you advice, though they are not always so amenable when they are taking you to task about breaking or bending the rules! You will probably be handed a leaflet which encapsulates the food regulations referring to markets, stalls marquees, tents, mobile canteens and vehicles as opposed to permanent premises, and based on the Food Hygiene (Market Stalls and Delivery Vehicles) Regulations, SRO 791 (1966).

Mobile Food Sales

You might also bear in mind the possibility of selling from a van instead of from a stall. A mobile wholefood shop or a delicatessen which takes delicious homemade food specialities to areas and villages where top quality food shops are remote could be a very profitable venture provided that you:

* have a clean driving licence and enjoy driving
* can raise the money to acquire and fit out a van
* ascertain beforehand where such a service would be most used
* advertise beforehand to inform your potential customers when you will be in their neighbourhood and what sort of goods you will have for sale
* get your costings right to make absolutely sure that they take into account all the running costs of your vehicle, including not only petrol but also taxation, insurance, maintenance, servicing and depreciation

Food Hygiene Regulations

The most significant of the food regulations that apply to market stalls and delivery vehicles (and differ from those applying to premises which have already been discussed) are listed below, but these are merely intended as a general guide. If you are planning to go into this sort of business seriously you must seek out more detailed information, including, perhaps, legal advice. The following points are taken from the Food Hygiene (Market Stalls and Delivery Vehicles) Regulations, 1966.

GENERAL REQUIREMENTS

* a food business must not be carried on at or from any stall, the condition, situation or construction of which exposes food to the risk of contamination, and no delivery vehicle shall be used which is so constructed or is in such a condition that the food is exposed to the risk of contamination
* every stall and delivery vehicle must be kept clean and in such good order, repair and condition as to enable it to be effectively cleaned
* every stall and delivery vehicle must have displayed conspicuously and legibly upon it the name and address of the person

carrying on that business, and any other address at which it is kept or garaged
• if open food is sold from a stall, other than from within an enclosed and covered market, the stall shall be suitably covered and screened at the sides and back so as to prevent any contamination of the food

PERSONAL HYGIENE
• a suitable first-aid kit must be provided at every stall and on every delivery vehicle in a readily accessible position and must include a sufficient supply of bandages, waterproof dressings and antiseptic

FOOD
• food consisting of meat, fish, gravy or imitation cream, or prepared from or containing any of those substances or any egg or milk must be stored at a temperature of below 50°F (10°C) or above 145°F (52.7°C) except where it is exposed for sale, or is brought to a stall within four hours before opening and will be exposed for sale when the stall opens, or is kept available for the replenishment of food of a similar kind which is exposed for sale. Food which is undergoing preparation, or movement from one part of the stall or market premises to another, or is being unloaded or loaded may fall outside the permitted temperature ranges provided it is restored to them as quickly as possible after completion of the process. The temperature requirements do not apply to certain foods such as bread, biscuits, cake, cooking fats etc
• no food shall be stored in any stall or delivery vehicle unless it can be kept clean and free from contamination

WASHING FACILITIES
• every stall and delivery vehicle must be provided with suitable and sufficient wash hand basins which must be conveniently accessible. Each wash hand basin must be provided with an adequate supply of hot water at a suitably controlled temperature, soap or other detergent, a nail brush and suitable means for hand drying
• every stall and delivery vehicle must be provided with suitable

and sufficient sinks or other facilities (not wash hand basins)
which must be kept clean and in good order and be provided
with adequate supplies of hot and cold water or of hot water at
a suitably controlled temperature

WASTE
* no refuse or filth must be allowed to accumulate on any stall or
delivery vehicle and adequate provision must be made for the
storage and disposal of waste

PENALTIES (Note carefully!)
* any person guilty of an offence shall be liable to a fine not
exceeding £100 for each offence or to imprisonment for a term
not exceeding three months or both. A daily penalty exists for
continuing offences

Group Catering in an Established Centre
Many cooks find that they make a little bit of money without
creating too many headaches by providing the amenity of a
restaurant or café in an established centre of some kind. For
instance, quite a lot of theatres, arts centres, art galleries and
museums, sports clubs and recreation areas want to offer refreshments to their members, customers or patrons because this is
good for business, brings in extra people and adds to the pleasure
of the place. However, they often don't want to employ extra
staff to run a catering service, and would prefer to offer their
facilities to an outside group, who are prepared to come in and do
their catering for them. This arrangement can be mutually
beneficial. The umbrella organisation provides kitchen and
restaurant facilities and customers. The catering group provides
food and drink, makes a profit if it is doing its sums and cooking
properly and pays a franchise, or a percentage of its profits, for
the privilege.

Many home-based, freelance women cooks find this an ideal
solution, if they can become part of a group. They can work part-
time, have the pleasure both of cooking and serving their good
food to satisfied customers, so that both their skills and their
need for companionship are fulfilled. Much of their preparation
and cooking can be done at home if they prefer so that they don't

have to neglect their families unduly. They can share in the joy of being part of a well-ordered business enterprise without having to worry about where the money is coming from to pay off such liabilities as rates, rents and electricity bills.

Nevertheless, there can be worries, even disasters, in this kind of arrangement. Sometimes the cooks disagree among themselves. They may feel that one of the group doesn't cook well enough, doesn't present her food with sufficient flair or isn't pleasant enough in her manner to the customers. There can be ill feeling if one woman seems to be asking for more time off than the others, wanting a lot of free Saturdays or not doing her fair share during the school holidays. And though most of these projects start off as group activities, based on democratic principles and governed by majority decisions reached by full and free discussion, it's surprising how often, despite themselves, they throw up a leader. If the leader is good, tactful, wise and diplomatic, that's fine. The organisation will probably be happy and trouble-free. But if the leader turns out to be aggressive, bossy, opinionated and tactless, it's almost certain that the group will eventually begin to disintegrate.

Quite apart from difficulties within the catering group, there may be problems between the cooks and the management committee of the organisation within which they work. As far as the cooks are concerned, if their takings are low they may think that the commission they are charged is too high or the franchise exorbitant. If customers are few and far between, they may come to the conclusion that the organisation's advertising and public relations activities are inadequate, and that they are being given a raw deal. Also, they may gradually become aware, through experience and the growth of their business, that the kitchen and restaurant facilities are somewhat inadequate and want to have better provision made for them. However, an arrangement of this nature is a two-way deal, and is bound to be something of a compromise, so the caterers must realise that the organisation has its problems too. I spoke to the manager of an entertainment centre and asked him about the difficulties he came up against as the member of staff responsible for the restaurant, which functioned on a commission basis rather than a franchise agreement:

'We have special problems,' he said. 'I can think of no less than six which have been exercising my mind recently. We operate in a redundant church which was not tailor-made for the things that happen in it today. So, our kitchen facilities are not good enough for the cooks to make their dishes on the premises, and they have to cook at home in their own kitchens. There are eight of them, all cooking on different days in different places, so it's difficult for us to be sure that they're conforming with the health regulations laid down, though when they're here we are very careful that we all stick rigidly to the rules. Our storage facilities are meagre. We don't even have a deep freeze here. Consequently our wastage level is higher than it should be in a well-run restaurant. We never know exactly how many to cater for, you see. There are busy days and quiet days. Of course, the cooks can take home any of the leftovers, but if something's been frozen once it can't be frozen again, and few of them have families big enough to dispose of everything.

'The quality of the food requires continual checking to make sure that standards remain high. It's impossible for eight different women all to work to the same standard every week, month in, month out. There are bound to be fluctuations. Portion control is a headache too. We have to keep a careful eye on that. Once price ranges have been fixed by agreement between the cooks and the centre it's absolutely vital to get the portions right, otherwise it might make all the difference between eventual profit and loss. We also have to make sure that all the cooks agree about the general pattern and style of the restaurant – the format, appearance, food presentation, method of serving, all that sort of thing – and we must ensure that there is effective co-ordination between the activities of the restaurant and the other activities of the centre. It's possible that the aims of the cooks may be different from ours. Obviously they have different priorities and, unless we agree about what we are all trying to achieve, resentments can flair up on either side.

'We try to solve these problems through our meetings which we hold once a month. At each meeting we work out the cooks' roster, and inform them about any special activities that are planned in the centre, making absolutely sure that they are aware of our diary of events. This is very important if they are to do their preparation properly. For instance, if we hold a Christmas market or a beer festival, we might have hundreds of people in the building in one day. The cooks have to pool all their resources and work well ahead to make sure that they can supply enough refreshments for them. We also try to standardise any matters relating to quantity, quality and prices, which are thus under constant surveillance and review, discuss the provision of equipment and sort out their suggestions for any replacements, renewals, additions or improvements, trying to comply with their requests if we possibly can.

'As well as these regular and vital meetings, I am available, on a day-to-day basis, to talk to any cook personally if she's feeling worried or dissatisfied. Often just discussing a difficulty makes it much easier to cope with. Really, we have a non-stop, open and frank exchange going on between the cooks and the centre, a proper partnership and, as a result, we manage between us to run a restaurant that is well known and respected in the town as one which offers a high standard of well-prepared food. This is apparent not only in the number of local people who eat here regularly but also in the number of tourists and holiday-makers who are recommended to come and have a meal here by local residents, by their landladies and hoteliers and by the Tourist Office. We're a little bit off the beaten track, not central or easy to find, so they have to make an effort to discover us, but we are constantly amazed by the number of tourists who search us out, and who obviously find the effort has been well worth their while.'

Acquiring Your Own Premises

Frequently clever cooks think that the best way of making money from their skills is to find a little shop from which they can sell good homemade foodstuffs, both sweet and savoury, either to take away or to eat on the premises. Beware! This path is fraught with difficulties. The possibility of financial success might be quite high if you own suitable premises, if, perhaps, you have a centrally situated house on a busy thoroughfare and can turn one of your rooms into a little shop or café. This saves you the financial outlay of having to buy, or rent, and then maintain separate property, and the fact that lighting, heating, cooking and telephone bills can be shared between your domestic and your business life is an obvious plus factor. Also, it's usually convenient, though occasionally nerve-racking, to be able to work from home, especially for the woman with a growing family or dependent relatives.

Nevertheless, it's not all plain sailing, and there are some formalities to be observed, even in your own home where you may think you are absolutely free to do exactly what you want. This is far from the case. Unless the house has been used for a similar business venture before, you will need to apply to the local authority for 'change of usage'. If this is eventually granted, and it's bound to take time because the workings of bureaucracy are always slow, you may feel that you have scored a minor triumph – only to find yourself faced almost immediately with an expensive rate reappraisal! Business premises are more highly rated than domestic premises. And your troubles are not yet over. Without doubt the environmental health officer will want to inspect your house, and he will probably have some very expensive suggestions to make about extra sinks and/or wash hand basins, hygienic work surfaces, easily cleanable flooring and – if it's a café, sandwich bar or restaurant you have in mind – adequate lavatories with hot and cold running water in each, for both customers and staff. The weights and measures people will be keeping an eye on you too, just to make sure that everything you sell is accurately weighed and labelled, with full details of where it was produced and by whom. You may sometimes feel that you are caught in a web of red tape and that every official is out to make your life as impossible as he can. I know the feeling well. In my business I suffered problems from honey that wasn't labelled properly, scales that weren't exactly accurate, flooring that had a join which I was told made it totally unhygienic, the lack of a cupboard in which my washing-up lady could hang her coat and inadequate washing facilities for my customers. Working on a shoestring and running a café that was more of a social amenity for the village than a breadwinner for me, I often felt that I was being hounded by faceless men who were totally dedicated to trivia. However, when I did manage to look at the process rationally, it became apparent that most of their demands and restrictions were part of a carefully planned control system designed to protect the consumer and society as effectively as possible from food poisoning, infection, malpractices and swindling.

Nevertheless, in my opinion the high rates that are levied, even on small businesses with a low turnover, are an entirely different matter, and one that should be very carefully reassessed. Many little shops and cafés perform an immensely valuable social service in providing personal contact, concern and conversation which the larger stores deliberately discourage. Often the people who run tiny businesses work long, hard hours for little financial return, but the personal satisfaction, which was often the original motivation, becomes eroded through financial burdens and bureaucratic harassment. Consequently, corner shops and cafés are closing down in their hundreds before the advancing army of hypermarkets, supermarkets and self-service stores, leaving their regular customers desolate. An enlightened government might consider offering them a subsidy to stay in business rather than putting up their rates, especially since, in some cases, the alternative to a friendly daily chat across the counter might be a visit to the doctor for a bottle of Valium!

The headaches involved in buying, renting or leasing premises are obviously worse than using your own, and you should cost your projected business turnover very carefully indeed before you decide on this course, preferably discussing it with the Small Firms Service first of all. Overheads can be huge, and increase all the time. In order to pay rent or mortgage, rates, insurance, fuel and telephone bills, cleaning and decorating costs, maintenance and repairs, you need to put a lot of money into your till all year round. To do this you need to be centrally situated, with good parking facilities, which also means that you will be highly rated. You will need to be a reasonable distance away from any strongly competitive shops providing a service very similar to your own. And you will probably need to advertise regularly, which is yet another expense.

Despite all these warnings, some freelance cooks run shops which thrive and find it difficult to keep up with the demand for their products. Much depends upon the sort of area in which you are situated and the market you aim at. For instance, if the neighbourhood is well populated by affluent and discriminating people who are prepared to pay realistic prices for quality ingredients, good, wholesome, imaginative cooking and high standards, then a top-flight delicatessen could well be a money-spinner. If your shop is situated in the centre of a business area, with a large population of shop and office workers in urgent need of a snack lunch, then you could build up a lucrative trade by supplying an interesting variety of sandwiches, pies and pasties, or cartons of salad. Again, success depends in the long run on researching the market, pin-pointing the need and responding to it imaginatively and effectively.

7
Marketing

Good efficient marketing is an important ingredient in successful catering. It can: keep **costs low**, keep the **quality of the final product high** and make the cook's **time cost-effective**. There are few general rules that apply to every catering enterprise. It depends upon:

* where you live and the shopping facilities in your area
* the sort of catering enterprise in which you are involved
* the size of your catering business
* other demands upon your time and your daily routine
* the amount of ready cash you have at your disposal
* the storage facilities you possess – either deep freeze for fresh foods or made-up dishes or cupboard space for long-lasting foodstuffs like sugar, pulses, preserves, as well as basic commodities like tin foil, kitchen paper and napkins
* what sort of transport you possess

But every cook should be looking for the right price and the right quality.

The Cash and Carry

As part of your initial research, you should examine very carefully every Cash and Carry Centre in your area. Any bona fide caterer can get a card for a Cash and Carry, and I didn't come across one who didn't use them to a certain extent at least. However, no two Cash and Carrys are the same. One may have an excellent butchery department, another may excel at rather specialised and exotic foreign foods, yet another might have a splendid cold room with a huge range of cheeses, butters and other dairy products. The answer, if you are situated in a place where you have several in striking distance, is to become a customer at two or three of them. Don't, though, make the mistake of thinking you should go to all three every time you do your marketing. That is ludicrously wasteful of time and petrol, and even if you save a pound or two on your bill you will eventually be worse off, because for a cook time is money. It's much better to make a beeline for the one which has the speciality you need for a particular party – a choice cut of meat, Norwegian goats' milk cheese or whatever – and top up from the shelves with anything else that's getting low, even if you have to pay a few pence extra for it than you would to a rival firm two miles away.

The Cash and Carrys are keen to have your business, so much so that they will occasionally send you promotional material to tempt you with their special offers. Read their leaflets carefully. It may well be that there are genuine and generous reductions on foodstuffs you regularly use and, if you have storage space and the available cash, it's worth stocking up and saving money in the long run. (Remember that nearly everything tends to get gradually more expensive anyway so, if you can manage it, it's nearly always worth buying in large quantities when the price is right.) On the other hand, there are bound to be less worth-while promotions clamouring for your attention, and you must make a genuine effort to resist anything you don't really want or need. One hundred tins of baked beans at the 'amazing, cut-back, once-in-a-lifetime, give-away price' of 5p a tin, or £4.50 the lot, may seem like a stupendous bargain, but only if you use a great many tins of baked beans in your personal style of cooking. And it wasn't an ingredient that loomed large in the recipes of any of the cooks I spoke to! So, learn to say no to temptation.

The Supermarket

Virtually every town now boasts at least two or three supermarkets and, because they are in strong competition with each other and are able to buy in vast quantities, their food prices tend to represent extremely good value. They, too, have their own specialities which are worth searching out. Where I live, one supermarket is extremely good at bread and bakery and has a range of delicious and cheaply priced French cheese. Another excels at its huge range of exotic and top-quality fruit and vegetables. A third manages to sell fruit juices of all flavours at less than Cash and Carry prices and to undercut them with its own brand of butter. I also discovered that there are some hours of the day, and some days of the week, when special offers are to be found and the '20p off' stickers flourish like flowers that bloom in the spring. This apparent generosity on the part of the manager actually arises from the requirement to date-stamp certain products. He can't take the risk of having on his shelves goods that state categorically 'sell by 22 May' if it happens to be 23 May, so, from 20 May or so he's probably working very hard to move them, and will do so by slashing their prices. In my own favourite supermarket Monday is always cheap-cheese day and those of us who are in the know flock in to buy full-fat soft cheeses from France, port wine-flavoured Cheddar, strong Italian Mozzarella and a host of other perishable goodies, including such delicacies as taramasalata, satsiki and goats' milk yoghurt. It also pays dividends to visit the cold cabinets about one hour before closing time because suddenly bacon, sausages, pâtés and cold meats suffer vast reductions.

There are at least two other sources of valuable bargains, quite apart from the supermarket's special offer of the week or month, which will probably be heralded in the local paper. The first is the shelf or trolley on which staff put goods which have been slightly damaged, usually to be sold off at half price. The damage is always to the packaging, not to the product itself, so there is no danger in buying them, provided that they are going to be used up quite quickly. Here you will find dented tins of consommé or tomato purée, punctured bags of flour or expensive, crunchy, wholefood cereal that can often form an invaluable ingredient in your baking of cakes and biscuits, cling film or foil in tattered boxes, jars of expensive preserves that have lost their labels. The second is the deep freeze section. Just occasionally, bags of fruit or vegetables burst as they are put in by the shelf-fillers or man-handled by customers. When this happens it is customary for the supervisor to pop the lot into an extra protective bag and reduce the price forthwith.

It's well worth getting to know your local supermarkets like the back of your hand. Know their strengths and weaknesses. Know how their prices compare not only with each other but also with the Cash and Carry and the small shops. Know when they are likely to have bargains and where they are likely to be found. When you are beginning your catering venture get into the habit of popping in at all times of day, prowling around, keeping your eyes wide open and your mental calculator busy. If in doubt, jot down some of their basic prices so that you always have a check list to use for comparison when you are examining the price structure of a rival concern. Remember, though, that prices often change from week to week so that the process of keeping them under review is a continuous one. Some help is to be had from the BBC which often gives news of fluctuating prices, gluts, scarcities and good or bad harvests, which affect the shopper's spending power. Part of Jimmy Young's morning programme on Radio Two on Thursday is devoted to food marketing and, since a lot of cooks work with the radio as company, this is one way of gaining invaluable information without losing time.

The Small Shop

It is commonly considered that small shops, buying in small quantities and therefore necessarily at quite high prices, are of little use to the caterer who is trying to market economically. In fact, my research showed that this was not the case. Very often caterers established happy and mutually profitable relationships with the small shopkeeper who provided them with specially selected high-class produce at reasonable prices. They built up a basis of mutual trust and reliability from which each was able to benefit financially, and along with this there was often the spin-off of professional respect, understanding and even lasting friendship. 'I always go to Mr Crouch for my vegetables,' explained Anne, a dinner party cook who specialised in Mediterranean dishes. 'He knows exactly what I'm looking for and when he goes to the wholesaler he keeps his eyes open especially for me. For instance, he knows exactly when to buy aubergines. One week, when I'm longing for them, he'll say "No, no. Not ripe yet". The next, it'll be "Wait, wait. The price is too high". Then, just when I'm getting absolutely desperate, he'll produce them, perfect quality, marvellous price, and I can buy a whole lot. Some I use fresh. Others get made up into moussaka, aubergines provençales, stuffed aubergines and so on, and stashed away in my deep freeze. He's quite happy, you see, because I buy a great deal of stuff from him and I'm a regular customer, week in, week out, so he always keeps his mark-up as low as possible, and I trust him implicitly. I know he'd never try to do me. He's even become very involved in my dinner parties, always wants to know whether they've been a success, and how a particular dish was received. One of these days I've promised that I'll get him put on the invitation list as guest of honour and he can taste the end product for himself. He really deserves it. Recently, we had a great to do about mushrooms. I wanted to do a special mushroom recipe and I wanted field mushrooms, not those artificially cultivated apologies. He couldn't get any anywhere. I knew where they were growing – we live way out in the country – but I couldn't find time to get out there and pick the blessed things, and time was pressing on. In the end, Mr Crouch got a couple of kids to go out there and gather as many as they possibly could and deliver them to my doorstep on the very morning of the party. They couldn't possibly have been fresher, and they tasted superb as a finishing savoury, just tossed in melted butter with lemon juice and herbs. And, do you know, he wouldn't even charge me for them. Just asked me to give the boys a small tip for their time and trouble. That's service, you see. And friendship. You'd never get that in a Cash and Carry or supermarket!'

Anne's story was not unique. I heard other tales about splendid family butchers who scoured Smithfield for prime lamb or succulent pork, or even learned new methods of cutting and boning to satisfy their clients' needs. I was told about a little delicatessen which made supreme efforts to get special foreign cooked meats and cheeses. And health food shops where the owners actually taught newly fledged caterers the secrets of appetising wholefood cookery.

The small shop is still alive and well in many parts of the country and if you find a good one, with an owner you like and can trust, it's well worth giving him or her at least some of your custom, not just for the little bits and pieces and extras that bring in meagre profit, but for essential ingredients that you buy in quantity. A couple of lemons and three pounds of potatoes aren't going to make much of an impact on a greengrocer's takings – but it's possible that a crate of aubergines is.

The One-Man Producer

Closely allied to the small shopkeeper is the one-man producer who often raises and sells his own produce without the benefit of a middleman. When I was running 'Downton Coffee and Crafts' several of these people approached us, and usually we were pleased to do business with them. We bought our potatoes, sprouts and eggs direct from the local farmer, and in the summer his fields yielded strawberries and raspberries galore which we used fresh for afternoon teas and luncheon desserts, as well as made-up into puddings. We were able to work with the farmer to our mutual advantage. During the soft fruit glut we let him set up a trestle table in front of the café, and from there we sold punnets of fruit for him without taking any commission or rent. It was a small kindness, but one which he appreciated, and it often brought us extra customers, so it was a fringe benefit as well.

There was also a producer known universally as 'the ham man' who reared his own pigs and then sold us superb home-cured ham which he delivered direct to our door. His ham was certainly more expensive than the equivalent cut we could buy in the supermarket, but the flavour was superb and we rapidly became well known for the excellence of our ham salads and sandwiches.

We also had a friendly lady who ran a smallholding in the village. It was not much bigger than an allotment really, but she always let us know when the first young peas were ready or when the French beans were at perfection, and brought us tiny succulent carrots that tasted quite different from anything out of a freezer. Herbs were her speciality, and it gave her a great deal of pleasure knowing that we would actually use them in our cooking and sell the surplus in our shop, and she was always immensely grateful that we provided her with an outlet that allowed her to keep on gardening. Unfortunately she never made much money out of us, but obviously it was enough to keep her sufficiently motivated to do the one thing in the world she most wanted to do – exercise her green fingers.

It may be, of course, that you are a keen gardener yourself, and if you have time and space to cultivate this hobby, it's not only economical but also very beneficial for your standards of freshness and excellence to use garden produce whenever possible. My group of three partners plus one cook used to be able to provide for our café – when the season was right – our own lettuces, radishes, cucumbers, tomatoes and courgettes, figs, apples, pears, plums, blackcurrants, redcurrants and even asparagus. Our customers were always enchanted by the thought of eating our own produce, knowing that it was organically grown, unpolluted by chemicals and unjaded by time or travel. But it's not every caterer who has the opportunity or inclination to grow his or her own food, has a smallholding on the doorstep or even a selection of first-rate, co-operative small shopkeepers.

The Market

Markets are exciting, lively places and are fun to shop in, but the stalls can be extremely variable. Take any two selling the same sort of product and you'll almost certainly find huge variations in price and quality. And it's not always the case that you necessarily pay more for the best. There's often a smooth operator trying to con as much as he can out of your purse in return for any old rubbish he can possibly foist off on you. So, before you buy, watch, listen and ask a few questions. Local people know the good, trustworthy stalls – they're the ones that always have a throng of customers around them. And it's up to you to have eyes like a hawk. Insist on having the fruit and vegetables you can see on display, not the stuff dragged up from the bottom of the box. Don't be afraid to argue, even haggle. In the market place this is the breath of life. If they won't sell you the specific goods you want, buy elsewhere. They need your custom and they're surrounded by competitors, so it's very much a buyer's market, provided that you can resist their seductive patter, know exactly what you're looking for, what quality you insist on and what

you're prepared to pay for it. One final warning. Shopping in the
market place can be hugely enjoyable but it can also be time-
consuming and nerve-fraying. If you need comparative peace to
think and calculate, if you need room to manoeuvre a shopping
trolley, time and quiet, go back to your Cash and Carry or supermarket, and choose a time which is not a peak shopping hour.
Early in the morning is good, from 9am till 10am or late in the
afternoon, and it's less frantic at the beginning of the week than
towards the end.

Wholesale Bulk Buying

Some co-operative groups I spoke to, or occasionally single
caterers or small partnerships who had built up close, friendly
and mutually supportive links with others in their area, did a lot
of bulk buying, either from specialised wholesale markets or
from businesses which tended to pack and sell their goods in
large quantities. One of the group would take a van and go to
London or their nearest major centre and buy sacks of rice,
pulses, beans, flour and sugar, huge jars of honey and molasses,
gallons of wine vinegar and so on. Some who were brave enough
would contact their local farmer or meat market and buy whole
lambs or pigs or half a cow, and do the butchering themselves.
Others bought fruit and vegetables by the crate or sack.

   This practice does save money. It has been estimated that a
food-buying co-operative can save from 15 to 50 per cent on their
food bills. It can only succeed, though, if you possess certain
assets including:

* suitable transport
* ample storage facilities
* sufficient time to spend on the lengthy business of the subsequent dividing up of the goods into smaller quantities for
  redistribution
* sufficient knowledge to enable you to break down the purchase
  into usable quantities for the benefit of the group (have you
  ever tried to butcher a lamb on the kitchen floor?)
* absolutely accurate scales
* a totally committed group of buyers who won't lose interest

and back out of the scheme (it needs to be reasonably big and constant to be viable)
- a group of buyers who will pay promptly and not keep you waiting for the money, since you will probably have made a cash transaction

A food-buying co-operative doesn't always work. One group I spoke to told me they spent so much time in collecting, weighing-out, repackaging and redistributing that there were hardly sufficient hours left for the actual cooking, so the purchasing power they gained was rapidly evaporated and the exercise was counter-productive. Before you get involved in this sort of exercise it would be wise to conduct your own time and motion survey or to give yourself a three-month trial period to find out if it really does work. It might, but don't count on it.

Your marketing habits depend upon your temperament. If you have the time and love the excitement and challenge of shopping, of sniffing out bargains, snapping up the exotic, unusual or unexpected, then the town centre is your oyster. If shopping is a dreary chore which you loathe and want to get over and done with as quickly as possible, then you will no doubt take an entirely different line and make it as painless as possible, even if you pay more in the process. Don't worry. If the extra expenditure saves your sanity, it's money well spent. The point about cooking for cash is to enjoy it and to eliminate or minimise those tasks which give least pleasure.

8
Organisation

It has been stressed throughout this book, and it emerges in almost every interview in chapter 10, that for the freelance cook time equals money. To make your time thoroughly cost-effective it's essential to be well organised. Organisation is required in five areas of your operation: **bulk buying, bulk cooking, pre-planning** for an event, the **management** of the event itself and the **administration** of day-to-day financial and business matters – keeping tabs on your labour force, cash flow, bills, invoices, insurance, advertising, future bookings and so on.

Bulk Buying and Cooking

Both of these matters have been dealt with in earlier chapters, but just to refresh your memory, remember that it's important that:

* whenever you do either you should be working not only for the immediate event in hand but also putting aside supplies for those coming up in the future
* it makes financial sense to take advantage of any glut or bargain offer so that goods can be stored for the time when they may be in short supply or more than usually expensive. Don't forget that even those things like lettuce or cucumber which can't be frozen in their natural state can be cooked and kept in the deep freeze
* even the busiest and most successful cooks have quiet spells, and these should be used to fill the freezer, to make tins of biscuits, to bottle fruit, preserves or pickles, and to sort out paperwork, publicity and preplanning
* nearly every cook is presented with emergencies from time to

time; a booking for fifty suddenly escalates into a request for food for seventy-five or a valuable customer asks for a special dish for a dozen unexpected houseguests at less than twenty-four hours' notice. You should always have sufficient resources and reserves to be able to rise to such a situation since it will probably pay dividends in the long run, by building up both your reputation and your clientele

Preplanning for an Event

The success and financial viability of a function will depend very largely upon the care you take with planning. You should always try to persuade potential customers to give you as much notice as possible. If you have a month or two to make your plans there is more chance that you will be able to:

* acquire all the foodstuffs you need to provide a really exciting menu at the right price
* gather together the best possible team of helpers, if help is needed, both for serving and clearing up, and to provide services like flower arrangement and entertainment
* fit in two or three bookings at about the same time without having to concentrate all your forces at the last minute on one rushed job
* enjoy the work involved without being harassed to death by the fear that you may not be as efficient and well prepared as you would otherwise have been

It may be that your first contact with a would-be customer will be a request to quote a range of prices and sample menus for a certain number of people on a specific day. At this stage it is very important to be efficient and business-like. Don't take long to make your quote. If other caterers get theirs in first you may lose out, even if yours is more favourable, simply because the customer is getting into a panic about confirming all the arrangements. This is especially the case with weddings when there seem to be so many things to organise. Besides, delay in putting in a tender is bound to minimise confidence. The client can't be blamed if he or she comes to the conclusion that you may be tardy or inefficient over the actual organisation of the event. For the same reason you should make sure that your stationery and menu lists look smart and professional, clear and well presented.

If your quote is accepted, the next job is to meet your customer and finalise the arrangements down to the smallest detail, including:

* the exact composition of the menu and whether there are any special dietary requirements to be catered for; for instance, it's almost imperative these days to include a few vegetarian dishes, and it may be that some should fit in with Jewish or ethnic requirements too
* the number to be catered for
* the equipment that you are expected to provide, and whether there will be any extra charge for this
* the time of day when the food is to be delivered and served
* the time of day when you and your team are able to get into the house or hall where the party is to be held
* how, where and by whom the clearing up and washing up is to be done, and whether there is a dish washer and/or plenty of hot water and tea towels
* what time your part in the event is likely to end

If you can possibly see the venue and the kitchen premises at this stage it will help enormously. Take careful note of things like power points, the size of the ovens, warming cabinets, refrigerators, the amount of preparation and storage space available, as well as waste disposal. Often something as cheap and simple as a large plastic sack in which to collect up wrapping, packaging and leftovers can save hours of trekking about gathering up the debris.

Having had your detailed discussion with the host/hostess and made your scrutiny of the premises, you need to get down as much as possible in writing. Have a notebook in which you can enter on one page what is available in the way of equipment and facilities, and on the facing page jot down a list of what you will need to take with you. When you get home write immediately to your client to confirm your spoken agreement in black and white, and keep a copy for yourself (each copy to be signed by both partners) so that you both know precisely what you have agreed to. If there have been misunderstandings or omissions this is the time to get them sorted out, not when the party is in full swing. The written, signed and duplicated agreement should include the following points:

- date of the function
- number to be catered for
- menu and any special requirements
- charge per head, taking very careful account of the hours of labour involved, as well as food and equipment
- time of the caterer's arrival or 'get-in'
- time of the serving of the food, if this is to be done by the caterer
- time when the caterer's work is likely to end
- place where the party is to be held, and where the preparation, cooking and cleaning up are to be done
- any extra requirements, such as wine, music, entertainment, flowers, photographs
- date of payment, and whether part of the fee should be paid in advance, both to help the caterer with initial expenses and to serve as a deposit in the event of a cancellation

Though this type of organisation may seem fussy and over-formal, it adds to the smooth running of any function. It helps maintain friendly relations between customer and caterer since they both know exactly what is expected of them. And it minimises the risk of the sort of disasters some cooks described to me, such as arriving at a venue and finding that there weren't even any trestle tables provided or that they had been expected to do the flowers and had omitted to do so. Finally, it saves time and money in that it eliminates lots of follow-up telephone calls or visits.

Once you know exactly what is required of you, you can begin your preparations, shopping and cooking, and collecting together your team of helpers. If you have been wise in planning your menu, you will have agreed on quite a lot of dishes that can be cooked in advance, and only things like salads or filled vol-au-vents will need to be completed on the day itself. Make quite sure

that you don't leave yourself with too much fiddly finishing off at
the last moment, otherwise you will feel flustered and at a
disadvantage just when you need to be in complete command.
To achieve this you may need to make a very early start. Several
cooks told me it wasn't unusual for them to get up at two or three
o'clock in the morning to prepare a luncheon or early afternoon
engagement.

A successful caterer will, however, be prepared to do much
more than simply provide the food and drink. He or she should
be able to offer several other related services, such as organising
the decorations, entertainment and gifts for children's parties or
have a network of contacts who can be recommended. You
should know, from personal experience, who works well and
does a good job in any of the areas connected with catering, and
discuss some sort of mutual help and recommendation with
them. The sort of expertise you are looking for lies in the field of
entertainment for:

- children, eg conjurers, clowns, magicians, ventriloquists,
  Punch and Judy operators, fireworks experts
- teenagers, eg discos
- other age groups, eg after-dinner speakers, compères, toast
  masters, cabaret acts, small bands, pianists, singers

You should also be able to call upon: **photographers,
lighting experts,** both in external flood lighting and special
interior lighting effects, **marquee hirers** and **wedding cake
decorators.**

Don't be satisfied with knowing only one of each. They may
well have another booking just when you need them. Try to find
two or three experts in each field and keep their details (name,
address, telephone number(s), what they do, what they charge,
past successes which you have shared) in a contact book so that
you can always get in touch with them easily. A small looseleaf
folder or file is best for this, the different categories entered on
different pages in alphabetical order.

ENTERTAINERS (CHILDREN)

MARK and MARGIRA Magicians
  10 The High St., Amersham
  Tel: 0000

  30 minute act. Fee £20
  Beswick Staff Children's Party
  Mrs Oglethorpes's Christmas Party
  Well received. Good standby for
  short notice.

TICKLISH ALLSORTS General entertainers
  7 Steel Way, Buckingham
  Tel: XXXX

  1 hour act, variety. Fee £60
  Very experienced, very popular.
  Recent TV appearance.
  Need 2 months' notice.

WILLIAMS, Ron   Punch and Judy
  19 The Avenue, Anderton Village
  Tel: 00XX

  20 minute act. Fee £15.
  Very popular.
  Only available during winter because
  of summer season commitments.
  Great success at Xmas parties 1982.
  Highly recommended.

CAKE DECORATORS

ANDERTON, Jennie
  17 Love Lane, Wendlesham
  Tel: 0X0X

  Charge: £75 for three-tier fruit cake.
  Very professional. 20 years' experience.
  Specialises in wedding cakes, will do
  others.

CHANCE, Verity
26 The Common, Moortown
Tel: X0X0

Charge: £60 for three-tier.
Comparative beginner. Still
going to classes. Attractive, less
traditional designs. Very highly
recommended by Browns for
21st birthday order.

JONES, Bob
The Hollows, Wintersway
Tel: XX00

Charge: £15 for decorated sponge.
Novelty cake, especially suitable
for children and teenagers, only
requires 2 days' notice.

Caterers' business agreements with their contacts are usually organised in one of three ways. They can look upon their local knowledge simply as an extra asset and recommend the services of their contacts to the client, hoping that their catering will be recommended in turn when the opportunity arises. For instance, if a firm organising a children's party as a treat for the families of its staff books the entertainment first, the chosen entertainer could easily suggest a caterer whom he or she has worked with successfully before, and that could be you. This is a form of mutual self-help widely practised by freelance workers, and it can be very beneficial and profitable. But you must only recommend someone you know to be good and reliable, otherwise your recommendations will rapidly be seen to be worthless. Another way is to recommend, and if the recommendation is taken up you can then act as an agent and charge the person for whom you have secured the work a small fee or commission. Needless to say, this has to be worked out between you beforehand and some agreement arrived at! A third way is to sub-contract the services of your contacts and employ them for the event. In other words, the total bill is paid to you, and you then pay the entertainer, photographer and/or cake-maker the fee that has originally been offered and accepted. There are benefits and drawbacks to be considered before becoming involved in this sort of arrangement.

The main advantage is that you are in total control and can be quite firm about exactly what you want from those who are working for you. This gives a cohesion and style to the event which can be very satisfying, especially if it is a grand occasion like a ball, where it is best to have the music, decorations, lighting and food complementing each other instead of clashing. The main disadvantage is that you take total responsibility. If the photographs are bad, you will be blamed. If the band plays too loud, it will be your fault. And if your customer pays late, or even not at all, it will be you who will have to sort out the finances with the others.

There is no easy answer as to how you should work with your contacts. Some of the cooks I interviewed were so adamant that they wanted to do things their own way that they would only use sub-contractors. Others were equally decided that their job was the food, nothing else, and they refused to be diverted by having to give time and attention to any of the other attractions. It seems to be a matter of temperament and preference.

It seems to me, though, that most caterers should be able to provide floral decorations as an optional extra if required. Flower arranging is not a difficult art to master, and if you grow flowers, berries and greenery in your own garden it need not be expensive. In fact, it can be quite a profitable addition to your bill. You must, of course, charge extra because of the time involved, quite apart from the cost of any bought blooms, but it's certainly very satisfying to make sure that the flowers match the tablecloths, napkins and the colour of your cuisine.

As soon as your quote is accepted and your booking confirmed, you will be busy organising your food, marshalling any of the other services you are required to provide and getting together your team of helpers, whether they are friends, family or acquaintances anxious to share in the fun and get involved. It's surprising how many people positively enjoy this kind of work as a hobby. Bank managers, theatre sisters, postmen, milkmen, chartered accountants, butchers, builders – all of these, I have discovered, are busy from time to time being part-time butlers, waiters, barmen and washers-up. The helpers are there for the asking. You only need to give them two things. The first is a pre-arranged fee. This may be minimal, but a lot of people like to earn a little bit of extra money, and it prevents them from feeling used or put upon and you from feeling obligated. Secondly, and most important, you must provide a happy working atmosphere. Friendly respect, appreciation and companionship will mean that they find fun in what they are doing and will do it well. A satisfied team tends to work well and confidently and imparts a feeling of good will and pleasure to the guests; this atmosphere of easy friendliness and efficiency, the rapport that every caterer should be aiming for, can really make a party.

The Management of the Event

To make sure that everything runs smoothly when the event is in full swing you must have made your preliminary arrangements precisely. You must also give yourself plenty of time. It's wise to calculate very carefully and methodically exactly how long it will take you to lay out the food and do the final garnishing, preparation and presentation, and then allow a good extra margin of time in order to cope with any last-minute emergencies that might crop up. It's much better to be ready too soon than to keep guests waiting.

You should also have briefed your helpers properly so that everyone knows exactly what they are supposed to do. Don't find yourself in the situation where some tasks are performed twice over and some neglected completely, or where some of the team are rushed off their feet while others stand around feeling unemployed and bored. And it's wise to cultivate the art of graceful delegation. If you ask someone to help you must give them a certain amount of responsibility. Try not to feel that you, and you alone, are capable of laying the table or arranging a tray of canapés. It's one thing to check other people's work tactfully and discreetly, it's quite another to do it for them.

It is another basic but necessary precaution to make sure well in advance that your transport is functioning properly, is clean, ready for loading and topped up with petrol. The loading itself must be done carefully because it's vital that everything goes in, in the proper order. It may waste hours of precious time if necessary equipment, or some of the food, is left behind or put in the wrong place and consequently mislaid at the other end.

The only way to master all these details is to make lists. Peter Combes, who runs the complex and highly successful 'Nadder Catering', told me, 'I am a fanatical list maker. I make lists for absolutely everything. You must always make lists.' His advice is sound. Whenever my own business took on an outside catering engagement I automatically compiled the following lists:

- work to be done, when and by whom in the days leading up to the event
- jobs to be done, at what precise time and by whom on the day itself
- equipment (cutlery, crockery, vases, candles and candle-holders, cloths, tea towels, napkins, plus extras to cover such emergencies as breakages or loss) that needs to be transported, and whether some of this should be taken the day before
- food, either prepared or ready to be made up on arrival, that needs to be transported (and I also made sure that the food was in spillproof, crushproof and labelled containers to avoid confusion on arrival)

This sort of methodical approach is sensible whether you are in the business of providing small dinner parties or large-scale banquets, children's picnics or village weddings. It is also necessary, on a day-to-day basis, if you are planning to run a small shop, café, delicatessen or freezer food take-away. At the beginning or end of each day you should make your plans, do your checks, write your lists, think and prepare beforehand for the actual job in which you are involved, that is, the job of selling food for a profit.

Administration

All this detailed catering planning is supported by a structure of longer-term planning – the organisation of insurance, accountancy and advertising, the payment of tax, the settling of bills and the planning of the budget. No successful business of any size can be run without a great deal of paperwork these days. At the core of the paperwork are two important ledgers: the **cash book** and the **petty cash book.**

The Cash Book

This shows all your income and expenditure on a daily basis. Usually it will deal with a month's business on one double page. The date and the various sources of income are entered on the left-hand side, the expenditure on the right, so that you can see at a glance if they tally effectively. If the income columns are looking sparse and the expenditure columns crowded, investigate carefully to make sure you're not overspending unduly, though there's no need to panic about temporary cash flow hiccups if you

RECEIPTS AND BANKING

DATE	SHOP SALES		CAFE SALES		CATERING SALES		TOTAL BANKED	
JULY 1	40	15	30	60	–	–	70	75
2	38	60	25	25	–	–	63	95
3	42	65	18	20	120	00	180	85
5	25	40	25	20	–	–	50	60
6	39	80	15	30	–	–	55	10
7	35	55	21	75	–	–	57	30
8	27	40	25	00	40	00	92	40
9	39	15	23	65	–	–	58	80
10	38	20	31	25	30	00	99	45
12	23	80	24	90	–	–	48	70
13	28	70	32	60	–	–	61	30
14	32	40	29	30	–	–	61	70
15	33	10	26	45	–	–	59	55
16	26	50	28	00	150	00	204	50
17	34	15	36	30	–	–	70	45
19	22	55	25	15	–	–	47	70
20	21	90	32	10	–	–	54	00
21	28	20	30	65	–	–	58	85
22	31	60	32	45	–	–	64	05
23	28	10	30	25	–	–	58	35
24	34	55	35	60	20	00	90	15
26	20	40	22	15	–	–	42	55
27	22	85	25	25	–	–	48	10
28	21	90	30	15	–	–	52	05
29	28	85	29	45	–	–	58	30
30	33	45	30	15	–	–	63	60
31	35	80	32	65	–	–	68	45
	831	70	749	85	360	00	1941	55

BANK PAYMENTS

DATE	PAYEE	CHEQUE No.	TOTAL AMOUNT	FOOD PURCHASE	RENT+ RATES	LIGHT+ HEAT	TELEPHONE + INSURANCE	VEHICLE	PRINTING + STATIONERY	ADVERTS	REPAIRS + RENEWALS	SALARIES	SUNDRIES	DETAILS OF PAYMENTS
JULY 1	Youngs Cash Carry	03185 1	116 95	116 95										
3	Cash	2	75 00									75 00		
5	Cash	3	50 00										50 00	Petty Cash
7	Southern Electricity	4	46 16			46 16								
9	Smith Greengrocer	5	26 40	26 40										
11	Tantivy D.C.	6	240 24		240 24									Rates
15	Ace Printers	7	21 70						21 70					
21	Jones Garage	8	64 25					64 25						
23	British Telecom	9	115 20				115 20							Telephone
25	Browns Timber	03186 0	24 60								24 60			
26	Youngs Cash Carry	1	154 15	154 15										
30	Tantivy Times	2	25 70							25 70				
			960 35	297 50	240 24	46 16	115 20	64 25	21 70	25 70	24 60	75 00	50 00	

The Cash Book

have an understanding bank manager and overdraft facilities. Long-term cash flow problems are more worrying and should be examined and discussed, probably with your accountant, before they lead you into real trouble. Printed here is a sample of one month's typical cash book entries for a small catering business with income from a shop, café and outside functions. With different types of businesses the column headings will vary, but you can adapt these to your own requirements.

The easiest way to keep your cash book well organised is to fill in what money comes in, and what goes out in cheques, as and when it happens, but if you hit a particularly busy period and can't cope with it on a daily basis, keep all your receipts, bills and invoices carefully together, making sure that they are clearly dated, and enter them up at the end of the month. Never delay longer than that because it is a fact of life that, no matter how painstaking you try to be, pieces of paper do get lost, you tend to forget exactly what you've been doing, and the whole thing gets into an enormous muddle and takes about three times as long to sort out.

The Petty Cash Book

Small amounts of money, paid out in cash, should be recorded as a lump sum in the cash book and then broken down into small detail in the petty cash book. Again, it makes life easier if you enter your spending daily, but if you can't manage it don't wait too long and don't lose your till receipts. The figure below shows a typical month's entry from a caterer's petty cash book.

As well as keeping these two books up to date, you must retain, either for your accountant or for your own use when preparing your accounts for the tax inspector: all your **receipts,** all your **invoices,** all your **bills** for gas, electricity, telephone, rates etc, your **bank pay-in slips** and your **cheque book stubs.** In other words, for the purposes of proof and double-checking, you must keep a twofold record of all your income and expenditure on a daily basis. It means work, organisation and a professional, thorough business-like approach, but it is important and must not be neglected otherwise you might either run headlong into financial disaster or fall foul of the tax man and the law.

Date	Payee	Total	Food Purchases	Cleaning Materials	Repairs & Renewals	Post	Casual Labour	Vehicles	Heating & Lighting	Details of Payments
July 1	Timothy Hardware	6 17							6 17	Calor Gas
3	Mrs Green	5 00					5 00			
5	Scotts	1 76		1 76						
10	Hardings Butchers	9 10	9 10							
12	Post Office	1 50				1 50				
17	Jones Garage	10 00						10 00		
21	Do-It-Yourself Shop	4 22			4 22					
24	Cowdon Bakery	8 20	8 20							
26	Winden Cleaner	1 50					1 50			
		47 45	17 30	1 76	4 22	1 50	6 50	10 00	6 17	

The Petty Cash Book

9
Presentation

Nearly every cook I spoke to told me that the presentation of food was of paramount importance. This can be unnerving for the beginner who might think that presentation is some mysterious skill that must be decoded before any newcomer can hope to compete in the world of catering. In fact, it is not difficult and comes almost as second nature to anyone who enjoys cooking and/or eating good food. But it is important.

We all know what a large part the sense of smell plays in our enjoyment of food. There's nothing like the aroma of sizzling bacon to arouse a healthy early morning appetite. But the sense of sight is almost as vital, and it's a cliché to describe something very pleasing to the eye as 'good enough to eat' whether it's edible or not. As a cook your food must not merely look good enough to eat – it must look too good to resist.

You can achieve visual delight by giving attention to: **colour, texture** and **shape.** These will be achieved not only by the food itself, and its garnishing, but also by the serving dishes, cutlery and crockery, the tablecloths and napkins, the flowers and the arrangement of dishes on the table in order to create variety and contrast.

You will be wise to arrive at a 'look' that matches the mood of the event for which you are catering, just as you would choose to wear clothes to suit the occasion. One of the first lessons to learn is to make your tableware appropriate. Nothing looks more elegant for a formal wedding reception than a snowy, starched, damask tablecloth. A white background can accentuate the colour of the food dramatically, and will not clash with the clothes of the wedding guests. But for a barbecue or riverside picnic it would not only be out of place, it would also be thoroughly impractical. In such surroundings brown and white gingham or buttercup yellow seersucker would be more in keeping. Similarly, wooden platters or chunky pottery bowls suit informal parties, while silver and sparkling glass are desirable for formal ones.

It's not only a question of making the equipment suit the occasion, for it's also true that some foodstuffs look better in one type of dish than in another. For example, green salad is shown to better advantage in a deep wooden bowl than in a glass dish, but glass is the best receptacle for fruit salads and ice-creams. A silvery dish brings out the shine in an aspic jelly, and for some reason a shallow copper dish makes fish look absolutely superb. As a general rule, plain dishes are better than patterned ones because too much decoration looks fussy and distracts the eye from the most important matter in hand, the food. It's also important to use containers that are large enough, so that there's no impression of overcrowding and the food can be properly displayed and arranged; this also makes for easier and more elegant serving.

For a small dinner party you may want to add a special touch by doing clever things with the napkins, folding them into water-lilies, fans or crackers. If you enjoy it and are not rushed off your feet, that's fine, and may well earn you some gasps of admiration from the guests. But it is a very time-consuming operation, would be quite impossible for a large-scale event and is not really necessary anyway. Heavy, good-quality napkins, neatly folded and properly positioned, are perfectly acceptable. It depends entirely upon the occasion, your client's requirements and your own schedule. Often a hostess will quite enjoy making these finishing touches herself if she isn't tied to the kitchen and, if so, it's just as well to leave it to her and gain yourself extra time for food preparation.

Likewise, if you are responsible for the flowers, it's wise to keep to simple arrangements. Concentrate on delicate colours that will not clash stridently with the food, and make sure that the size and shape of the decoration is appropriate for its position. A huge arrangement in the centre of a dinner table is infuriating. Seated guests have to keep peering around it to talk to the person opposite with the result that it becomes a conversation-stopper and a social menace, no matter how beautiful. Table arrangements should be small or very slender, and sufficiently well balanced and stable not to topple over if they are inadvertently touched when the dishes are being passed round. Similarly, a tiny miniature of primroses or harebells would be quite wrong in a niche or corner which is crying out for something bold, colourful and eye-catching. Again it's a matter of common sense and thought. Flowers enhance any room, but they must be the right flowers in the right place. A single white rose is often more beautiful than two dozen dazzling chrysanthemums, as well as being less expensive to buy and much more cost-effective to arrange.

But quite apart from table linen, serving dishes and flowers, the food itself is the most important focus of colour, texture and shape. The majority of cooks, whether professional or amateur, instinctively create variety, even in the most humble of meals – golden flaky pastry set off with the smooth ivory of boiled potatoes, fresh green sprouts, bright carrots and rich brown gravy. It's unlikely that many of them would surround a suet pudding with the non-colours of butter beans, cauliflower and mashed potatoes. Similarly, most of us will automatically brighten up the delicate shades of rice and chicken with a colourful green salad, strips of red, yellow and green peppers or peas and corn. Colour is an appetiser, a fact well known to hospital nutritionists trying to stimulate unwilling appetites, so every menu should contain a colourful element – rich purple bortsch as a starter for a dinner party, tomato and pepper salads or aspic jelly floating with chopped parsley as part of a savoury buffet, cool, contrasting citrus fruits chopped up and served in shining glass for a sweet-sharp mouth-freshener. (It's a simple trick, but an effective one, to dip the rims of serving glasses first into lemon juice and then into rainbow sugar crystals to give a sparkly, textured finishing band of crunchy, edible colour.) The meal can end with a variety of cheeses of all shapes, shades and textures, red and yellow Edam, creamy Brie, garlicked cottage, blue-veined Stilton, golden Double Gloucester. The cheeseboard itself, carefully arranged on a wooden platter, can look as pretty as a picture. Think of colour contrasts when you're planning your menu and doing your shopping, and it will help you to create a beautiful table.

You can also add to the visual element of your food by using garnishes, but try to be more ambitious than simply using parsley with everything, and remember the two golden rules. All garnishes should be edible, part of the dish, and they should be chosen not only to beautify, but also to enhance the flavour. Sometimes a very delicately flavoured garnish highlights the delicacy of the recipe, as in the delicious combination of grapes with white fish. Sometimes a strongly flavoured garnish makes an exciting contrast to a rather subtle food, as is the case with cheese sauce and cauliflower. In these examples it's not only the two flavours, but also the two colours and the two textures that are complementary.

There are many types of garnish you can use, including: **sauces, vegetables, herbs** and **flowers, fruit, cheese, cream, chocolate, eggs, butter, mayonnaise, breadcrumbs, nuts, cereals** and **aspic jelly.** All have their place. A few of the more unusual ones you might like to try are as follows:

- dip wedges of lemon into finely chopped parsley and serve with kebabs, fish or chicken
- dip tomato quarters into parsley or Parmesan cheese and use to garnish cold meat or chicken
- put a slice of lemon on top of a slice of cucumber, cut almost to the centre, then twist the two halves into opposite directions for a pretty butterfly decoration for fish
- add chopped parsley to finely diced onion and spread the green and white speckled mixture over tomato salad
- hollow out tomatoes and fill with prawns in mayonnaise, then place in a bowl of lettuce
- make tomato 'flowers' by cutting off the top of a tomato, turning it upside-down on a chopping board and slicing it down in sixths, almost but not quite to the bottom. Open out the segments carefully so that it looks like a flower, and use it to garnish a tray of canapés or vol-au-vents
- make egg 'daisies' by piercing round the middle of a hard-boiled egg with a series of V cuts, using a sharp, pointed knife. Push it well into the centre each time, then gently separate the two halves to make two flower shapes (this can be done with tomatoes too)

- slice a hard-boiled egg in half lengthways, scoop out the yolk, mash up with mayonnaise and seasoning, return the mixture to the egg boats and use them to decorate a plate of cold meats
- make butter 'curls' by dipping a metal butter curler into hot water and dragging it along the length of a pack of butter. The curls will form underneath the tool, and should be piled into a dish and chilled before serving
- make butter 'balls' by cutting butter into small cubes. Rinse two ridged butter pats under cold water, put a butter cube between them, then rotate the top pat only, quite slowly, until the cube has turned into a ball. For variety of both flavour and appearance some of the butter could have herbs chopped into it. Butter curls and balls look very good as an accompaniment to the cheese board
- beat butter till soft, adding herbs, garlic, lemon juice and seasoning, then spoon into the centre of a square of kitchen foil, and close up the foil carefully, twisting both ends of it in opposite directions so that it looks like a silver Christmas cracker. Chill for several hours. When quite firm, unwrap the roll of butter and slice into rounds to be served on steak, chops, fish or vegetables, where they will melt and add a delicious flavour
- fry fresh breadcrumbs in butter until they are crisp and golden. Mix with finely chopped hard-boiled egg and sprinkle over cauliflower
- use fruit as a garnish for cold meats. Try apricot halves filled with mint jelly, or pineapple chunks dunked in chopped parsley
- use a potato peeler to make curls from a bar of plain chocolate and sprinkle over cream-topped desserts
- serve soft-textured desserts with very thin, crispy shortbread fans or fingers
- sprinkle finely chopped nuts or crunchy wholefood breakfast cereal over ice-creams or soft, creamy puddings. The contrasting flavour and crispy texture will complement the bland smoothness of the dessert

In the end, even though the food is beautiful, the garnishes colourful, the cloths and cutlery immaculate, the glass and china shining and sparkling, the final vital ingredient rests with *you*. Only if the cook and his or her team look good and behave well, will the presentation be perfect. The most delicious dish will seem tasteless if it is offered without grace. It's not only important for the servers to look smart and well groomed (whether they're wearing uniform or informal clothes is irrelevant and depends solely on the style you're striving for), it's also important for them to care, and to show they care, about the guests' well-being. Good manners, courtesy, smiling faces – all these should be part of the package you are presenting.

Almost every caterer I spoke to stressed that cooking for cash was very hard work, it could be worrying and it could be exhausting. Nevertheless, they all found immense satisfaction in using their skills to give other people pleasure, and found it a way of life in which there was an immense amount of fun. Let this sheer sense of fun be the final garnish, the essential flavour of your service, and you'll never be short of bookings.

10
Cooks Talking

'Lucy of Lewes'   Outside Catering Specialist

I was born profoundly deaf, and went to a special school. When I left, at about sixteen or so, I didn't really know what to do for a career. I spent a year or so working with horses, but there was obviously no future in that. In fact, there were about six possibilities open to me, so I discussed them all very carefully with my parents and we eventually decided that cookery would be the best thing. We approached the Cordon Bleu school in Marylebone Lane, London, and they were most kind. They suggested that I should have a week's trial period so that I could be assessed as a potential student. When the week was over they agreed to take me on for the full course, lasting a year, just as soon as I was eighteen. I was the first deaf girl they had ever trained and I was one of forty-eight students. The staff were all very sympathetic, helpful and supportive, and the other students were kind too.

It was a very hard course for all of us, extremely stiff. We all shed tears from time to time, but I suppose I had particular problems because I had to lip-read what was being said as well as watch what was happening and sometimes I missed things that were going on out of my vision. But I managed because if ever I got into difficulties there was always someone to give me a little extra help, to explain things.

At the end of the year I passed my examinations and got my certificate, and we were all delighted, my parents and all the family. My father and I then had to think what I should do next. Hotel catering didn't seem to be the answer. In an hotel or restaurant it's a very competitive world. I could have been stuck in the kitchen peeling potatoes. No one would have had the time to bother about my hearing disability, and there is no earthly reason why they should have put themselves out, anyway. I don't think I would have got on at all. So we decided that I should be self-employed, a freelance caterer. That was nearly ten years ago. Soon I shall be holding my tenth anniversary party for all my helpers, over fifty of them! And I shall cook all the food.

I began in a very small way. Friends and neighbours were very kind and ordered bits and pieces from me, the odd cake or a pudding. Nothing much, but it was a start. For the next two years I used tiny little diaries for my engagements. Tiny little ones. Now I have a huge diary, a great big one, with a page for every day. Luckily, that's how my business has grown.

After I'd spent a long time cooking single dishes, I was invited to do the food for a wedding. The first time I just delivered the food, but then, when I got another booking, I thought I would provide a complete service. That meant a lot more organisation. First, I looked around for helpers. I always do all the cooking myself – my business is called 'Lucy of Lewes' and Lucy does the cooking. But I needed people to help with some of the preparation, and the serving and clearing up. My mother and father help me a lot. They aren't cooks, although they do kitchen work sometimes, and they answer the telephone for me. That's one job I can't do for myself, but it's just about the only job I can't do. My helpers came from all over the place, all walks of life. I have a chartered accountant, a bank clerk, a butcher, a printer, a carpenter, even a magistrate. People really seem to enjoy being involved. Recently I moved and I had a wonderful builder who helped renovate the house. He was so nice, I said 'I wonder if you would like to help me cater for a wedding on Saturday afternoon?' and he jumped at the chance. I choose my helpers very carefully. Lots of people come and ask for work, but that's not the best way. I like to make the first approach and do the asking. And for each occasion I try to choose my team to suit the event. If it's likely to be a 'heavy' party with a lot of drink flowing, I like to have some burly men about me. If it's quite a quiet, sedate do I can use older people who might not be able to cope with anything too energetic.

While I was building up my team of helpers I realised that I'd need transport so I bought a tiny little mini-van. Now I drive a

Ford Transit! Then I got some china, plain white, from the surplus china shop. I like real china because it feels so nice. It's stronger than people think, and anyway it can easily be replaced if it's broken because I always have the same colour and design. To start with I bought fifty of everything, cups, saucers, plates, the lot. That was in the early days. Now we've got stocks to cater for 350, crockery and cutlery.

My first really big engagement came when I was asked to do a picnic for 250 people. That was hard work, but fun – 250 picnics, all packed up into little white carrier bags. And that turned out to be my lucky break because one of the women on the picnic was the wife of the administrator of a very big business organisation which has its headquarters near here, and they began to engage me to cater for all their special events – cricket teas, children's teas, employees' parties, all sorts of functions.

From then on I was very busy, and my business grew and grew. Eighteen months ago I opened a shop. I'm buying my own premises, right on the High Street. There's the shop at the front, a coffee room behind and a kitchen, all downstairs, and I live in the flat above. We've made a lovely garden too, and people can eat out there when the weather is good. So, as well as catering for functions, I now sell freezer take-away food from my premises – nearly all Cordon Bleu recipes, like chicken dijonnaise, fillet of lamb soubise, sauté of veal martini – as well as homemade cakes, meringues and biscuits. Or people can have a light meal on the premises. Often they come in for coffee and cake and go away carrying something special to eat at home. It's a good idea to have lots of different things going at once.

Most of the time I work at full stretch, seven days a week throughout the year. Sunday is my big day for clearing up after the weekend rush and preparing ahead. January and February are quiet as far as outside catering is concerned but people still have private parties and order casseroles and sweets. And then I am busy in my shop, cooking ahead, filling the freezer, catching up. The summer months are frantic. One day in July I did cricket teas for 350 and then two hours later I put on a full-scale evening meal for 500 in a marquee. On days like that I'm often up to begin work at 2 o'clock in the morning. I need to have plenty of advance warning, of course. I like to be able to start preparations two months ahead, but sometimes it's as little as a fortnight. And I can cope with emergencies if I have to because my deep freeze is always well stocked.

It costs a lot of money to provide all the food and equipment I need but I have a helpful bank manager and overdraft facilities of £5,000, though I've rarely used them. But I had to prove myself first of all. Once I was able to show the bank audited accounts of three years' successful trading they were delighted to be supportive. I don't know if they would have been so keen right at the beginning. Even now, when the work is flooding in, most of the profits are ploughed back into the business, buying more equipment, improving the premises.

I like things to look as good as possible. Style and presentation are all important. We always try to give the same image of informal professionalism. As well as the white china we have damask tablecloths. And the helpers wear a blue and white uniform. The women have blue skirts, white blouses and blue and white Liberty print aprons. The men wear blue trousers, white shirts and little bow ties of the same Liberty print. They look smashing, very fresh and attractive, but it also means that they can easily be recognised in the crowd if they are needed.

I've never done much advertising, apart from being in the Yellow Pages, but we always drop business cards wherever we go. And I get quite a lot of publicity because, being deaf, people seem to like the fact that I'm managing to make a go of it. Lewes has always been particularly friendly towards me and I'm surrounded by a helpful, supportive community. Some time ago I won the Duke of Edinburgh's Gold Award, and that was reported in the local paper. The Mayor apparently felt this was good for the town and thought he should show some form of approval, so the Town Council presented me with a special illuminated address. Even better, they later asked me to cater for their Centenary Banquet, which was wonderful.

One of the things I like about the work is that there is so much variety but, it's funny, I started by doing picnics and I'm still doing picnics, for Glyndebourne, which is quite near here. Customers come in and give me their orders. We talk about what they'd like and I pack up a special feast in a cardboard box. It might be chicken Bangkok, salmon mayonnaise, vacherin chantilly, that sort of thing. I supply the china, knives and forks for no extra charge, no deposit or anything, and they drop them in on the way back home. No, I've never been done. I trust people and they're always honest. Well, I have been done once. A sort of Walter Mitty character ordered a great feast for the races, a whole lot of stuff from all sorts of suppliers, and he didn't pay for any of it! That was a little problem, but our share of the debt he'd run up was so small it really didn't seem worth making a fuss about, so we just wrote it off.

We had another problem once, catering for a wedding reception for 150 people in the crypt of a London church. We took all our food and equipment and helpers there, and when we got in we found only 400 chairs stacked up in the middle of the space. Nothing organised for us at all. It was a frantic rush after that long journey to get everything ready in two hours flat, but we managed it somehow. Usually we like to see the place beforehand, and to talk everything over with the client so that we know exactly what they want. But all that takes time, and our time is money.

We don't present a packaged deal, all we provide is the food and the service. But we have all the contacts anyone might need, and can always make recommendations. When people want wine we direct them to a friend who has an excellent wine shop nearby. And we can give advice about the hiring of marquees, who will do flower arrangements, which photographer will do a good job. We don't sub-contract, we just recommend. We like to concentrate on simply making the food as good as possible.

Marketing and costing are very important. It's not just a simple business of buying the ingredients then doubling or trebling the cost. Some dishes take hours and hours to prepare and so time has to be carefully accounted for. It's the same with our buying methods. Really we just don't have time to go to Brighton's fruit and vegetable market, that would be too expensive in both hours and petrol. We tend to buy from local traders as much as possible. Fresh fruit and vegetables come from the local greengrocer. Most of our poultry comes from the local butcher, always fresh, never frozen. Turkey we get from a local turkey farm. If we have time, we pick apples in bulk from a local orchard. But most of the time is spent in the kitchen – a nice, big, ordinary, family kitchen, though it does have an Aga and two electric ovens – providing what the customer wants. Experience has taught me that what the customer wants is first rate food, well made from quality ingredients, and I just do my best to see her or she is not disappointed. I still tend to use almost all Cordon Bleu recipes. If you look on the bookshelf you'll see that *The Constance Spry Cookery Book*, published by Dent, is the one that is most used. Even the recipe for my Christmas pudding is Cordon Bleu, and I reckon I have 150 of those to cook to order before Christmas comes around again. It's a busy life!

Liz Tofield   Private Caterer/Manager of the Restaurant of Wilton House on the Estate of the Earl of Pembroke

I'm a New Zealander, though I've lived in Britain for years. My mother was very interested in cookery and was determined that I'd be a competent cook too, so she made me prepare the family meal once a week. It was very good training. Apart from that, my only tuition has been a mini Cordon Bleu course I did in France – and that lasted all of a fortnight! Now I have a daughter of eighteen, Alexandra. Her family training wasn't as systematic. She was just thrown in at the deep end and had to help out and do her bit whenever necessary. Now she's a very good cook and works with me at Wilton House during the holidays.

When I first came to London I shared a flat in Holland Park with five girls. I had to learn a whole new approach to food. New Zealand is so rich in meat – we're great meat-eaters – but in London there wasn't the same sort of quality or quantity. Anyway, I just couldn't afford it. I reckon I learnt 295 different ways to cook sausages! Sausages and plaice – that was our staple diet. The things we used to do to make ends meet! I remember buying mushroom stalks and peelings for sixpence a bag; I couldn't afford the actual mushrooms. In 1962 I got married and became an army wife, and off we went to Malaya. There was a lot of super produce there, marvellous basic ingredients. So the first thing I had to do was to get myself a cookery book so that I could cook something other than sausages and plaice.

I love cookery books and read them the way an actress reads

play scripts or a journalist studies research material. I find
Marika Hanbury Tenison very readable. She's the first one who
springs to mind so I suppose she must be my favourite. I read
Robert Carrier with pleasure, but also with a pinch of salt, and
find myself adapting his recipes to my own personal tastes. He's a
great showman when he's demonstrating. Graham Kerr, the
Galloping Gourmet, is another favourite, perhaps because I met
him in New Zealand. And I love all Elizabeth David's books. I
once won an award for my pâté and got two of her books as my
prize, and I treasure them. Prue Leith, too, I'd put on my list of
favourite cooks. She's an Australian and I always feel that my
sort of cooking is very similar to hers. I reckon her *Complete
Cookery Course*, published by Fontana, is very good value.

In Malaya I had a Chinese cook and that was super because he
taught me Chinese cookery and I taught him English. I don't do
many Chinese dishes now though, not professionally, because
they're so time-consuming. The actual cooking is very quick but
the preparation of the vegetables takes ages, and that's expensive
if I'm costing my time properly. I also learned Indian cookery in
Malaya. There was a good Indian restaurant and I asked them to
teach me how to make real curries. I used to go along to their
kitchen once a week and have a proper lesson.

When I was out there our bank manager was a bachelor. He
used to have to do a lot of entertaining, and I often acted as his
cook and hostess. I remember on one occasion I had to organise a
party for more than thirty people in honour of the local 'king',
Yang di Peruan, and he wanted bombe Alaska of all things. I was
only twenty-three years old and very inexperienced, and I knew
it had to be superb, so really it was a terrifying experience. I
wasn't even very skilful then you see, but by that time I had
managed to acquire two good cookery books, and my mother
used to send me the Australian *Woman's Weekly*. The recipes in
the Australian *Woman's Weekly* are very good, though expensive
in meat and dairy products, as you might imagine. I was self-
taught, but quite brave and adventurous; that was my strength, I
suppose. If a recipe didn't work out the way it should have done I
would just whip it up and make it into something else! I've
always been an instinctive cook. I cook by feel. If it looks all right
and tastes all right, that's fine by me. I never weigh anything; I

do it largely by guesswork. I just throw things in till the texture's right and the flavour's right. I'm all for easy, happy cookery.

When I came back to England from Malaya I came back to economical food. A lot of the things I wanted were still not readily available, so I began to grow all my own herbs for flavouring. And I'd take along my *Woman's Weekly* to the butcher and show him the pictures and say 'Look, this is how I want my meat cut'. And he was marvellous; he did it just the way I wanted.

The private catering business just crept up on me. Friends knew I could cook and began to ask me to do little things for their dinner parties. Then the whole thing snowballed and I've been doing dinner parties from scratch since 1974. I've never ever advertised. Every job that's come my way has been the result of personal recommendation. I set my price by charging for the cost of the ingredients, then adding what I consider a reasonable hourly rate for my labour, plus 10p an hour for electricity. Sometimes people say I haven't charged enough, but it's very difficult being hard headed about money with friends. I find it less embarrassing with people I don't know.

When a hostess first asks me to cook for her, either I present a few sample menus and let her choose what she wants or she tells me straight away the sort of meal she has in mind, and then we discuss it and come up with a joint decision. The whole organisation is very flexible. On most occasions I start cooking in my own home and finish it off in my customer's kitchen. On most evenings I'd probably stay to serve it up unless it was something simple like a casserole. I'd certainly stay if it was a roast. Sometimes I use my own equipment, sometimes I use stuff from the house. I have lots of nice casseroles and serving dishes that I collect, just like cookery books.

I find that most of my bookings are for dinner parties or buffets. I just need about two days' notice for a dinner party, a little longer, perhaps, if the menu is particularly elaborate. I'll take on a dinner for between four and eighteen people. The biggest buffet I've ever done was for 160 people. That took me two days' work. Mostly I work on my own, but there are one or two people I can call on to help me out. Alexandra is the first one I turn to. And she has an undergraduate friend who will help whenever she's at home. Then we have another friend in the village who sometimes joins us. I never need more than that.

Basically I do Mediterranean cookery. If I have a speciality I suppose it's boned and stuffed poultry. Both my husband and I were taught how to do that by our Chinese amah. He loves cooking too, and can do that for me if I'm pushed for time. Occasionally he will plan and cook a meal for us at home, and the fact that he shares my enjoyment of fine food adds to my own satisfaction in preparing it. Despite the fact that I have my own catering business, and work at Wilton House during the summer, I still love cooking for the family and entertaining my friends. I like eating out at good restaurants too, and that's useful because I pick up lots of tips and ideas, and compare the chef's work with my own efforts. In London my favourite restaurants are 'San Frediana' in Fulham, which serves Italian food, and 'Poon's' in King Street, Covent Garden, where it's Chinese.

Two years ago I was asked to manage the Wilton House restaurant and that's a full-time job. I leave home at 8.15 in the morning and don't get back till 7.15 at night. It's a long day, but I just do it from March till October. During those months I limit my private catering bookings; I just take them on if I really have my arm twisted. All the same, I can get home and my neighbour, Lady Devlin, will telephone and say 'Please can you do me a mousse for my supper party tomorrow?' and I just get stuck in and make it. I don't like to let people down, and I don't mind cooking in the evenings at home, even after cooking all day.

The restaurant and the private work fit together quite well. Sometimes I can do the marketing for both at the same time. Sometimes the restaurant staff will help me out with my own catering. But more important than that, it's made me better organised, more economic. I've learned how to make sure there's little wastage. We keep the standard of food high. We serve quiches, turkey breasts, scotch eggs and cold meats with a variety of salads. And there are meringues, gateaux and cheesecakes. Everything is made on the premises except for the bread rolls which come from a good local baker. We buy hams and cook them our own way, get local trout from the nearby fisheries and salmon from Lyndhurst. It's our golden rule that we don't serve chips with anything!

After two years the marketing has become quite straightforward because I know exactly where to go for what I want. For instance, I usually use a good, small greengrocer who can get me practically anything I need, though the market can be good for some fruits, like melons. I also go to the market's wholefood stall for fruits, dried fruits I mean, and nuts and raisins. The Cash and Carry has an excellent butchery department, and it's pretty good for cheese too, though we only sell a small range. Apart from that, I use the supermarket, just like a housewife looking after her family. Good supermarkets really do have both quality and price taped these days, it seems to me, because they're highly competitive and can keep their mark-up low through buying in such large quantities.

Accounting and costing are an important part of any catering enterprise. I do my own accounts for my private business, and I also do the books for the restaurant. Basically they come through me, and then on to the estate office, and that's where the bills are paid. So you see, I wear two quite different hats, one as private caterer and one as restaurant manager. One is my winter hat, one my summer hat, but each one helps me to wear the other more comfortably. It's a frantic life, hard work – but I love it.

Tim Charlton   'Dial-a-Cake'

When I left school I worked as a trainee cook in a hospital and did a three-year City and Guilds course in 'Cooking and the Catering Industry' under the day release scheme. I suppose you'd call the City and Guilds the poor man's Cordon Bleu! We covered just about everything you could think of, and at the end of it I was a qualified chef. But I still wasn't satisfied. I wanted as many qualifications as I could possibly get. So I went back on one of my days off every week to do a course in 'Design and Decoration of Flower Confectionery'. That was great. I enjoyed that, and got a credit. I still don't think of myself as having finished training. Next I'd like to do a course called 'Advanced Bread'. You never stop learning in this business. There's always something new to master, and I suppose I'm ambitious. I want to get on.

When I was twenty-three I decided to have a year in Australia, just to broaden my experience, and the most extraordinary thing happened. One day I was buying myself a car, and I looked across the street and saw a shop with a sign that read 'Dial-a-Cake'. I was amazed. I couldn't even think what it meant! But cakes were my business, so I wandered over, walked in, rang the bell and out came this amazing girl. Tall? She was huge! I'm not exactly short myself, but I'm telling you, she towered over me. Her legs reached up to my chest, honest. She must have been six feet four if she was an inch. And the clothes! Black fish-net tights, a kingfisher blue leotard, black monkey jacket and jaunty little black bowler hat. I'm not kidding!

Well, this amazing woman was Christine, one of the owners of the business, in partnership with her husband, Peter. They ran three linked operations: 'Dial-a-Cake', 'Dial-a-Flower' and 'Dial-a-Clown'. But it was the cakes that I was interested in. I thought, 'You never know, there might be an opening here for me.' So, Christine told me how they operated. It was a great idea, but basically quite simple. A customer would ring up and say 'I want a cake to celebrate my judy's birthday' or 'my bloke's new job' or 'my dad's retirement' and Christine, she was really the organising genius, would say 'Okay. Tell us all about him or her', as the case may be. She'd get the whole story of the person who was being given the cake – how old they were, their good points and bad points, their favourite colour, and music, what their interests were, where they lived and worked, what sort of things they liked doing, why the cake was being bought, all that stuff. Then she'd find out where the party was being held, what they'd be wearing, what size of cake was required, what flavour, what message would be appropriate, the lot.

Some of the messages were very simple – happy birthday, good luck, congratulations, that sort of thing, usually with the name attached: 'Many happy returns, Harry'. But some of them were really wild. Remember, it was Australia and the Australians have a weird sense of humour!

Next Christine and the customer would fix a price (the minimum would be about £16) and, once the deal had been agreed, she would get down to work. Her job was to write a special song to go with the cake, using all that information she'd got, and put the words to the music of a well-known tune. She had seven she used, things like 'Auld Lang Syne', 'Annie Laurie', 'Waltzing Matilda', old favourites. She could write up to fifty songs a day. Then she'd make a beautiful card, with the words on one side and the music on the facing page.

The chef would decorate the cake. The cakes were bought in plain, not made on the premises. There were always some ready with basic icing, just waiting for the final decoration. For a weekend, which was the busiest time, they might have fifty cakes ready to go, so their delivery time could be very snappy, as little as twenty minutes if they didn't have far to take them.

When the song and the cake were ready, the delivery team sprang into action. The team was made up of five girls and one man. The girls were all young and pretty, and dressed up just like Christine. The bloke was dressed up too – tight trousers, dashing Spanish hat, and he played the mandolin! If the person who was having the party was a girl, the man with the mandolin arrived to serenade her and present the cake. He'd burst in saying, 'Dial-a-Cake, Dial-a-Cake, Dial-a-Cake for Julie', or whatever her name was. Then he'd sing her her own song, which he had written out for him on the card, of course, give her a smacking kiss and present her with the cake, all flashing with sparklers which he lit just as he carried it into the room. It was great, really. If the recipient was a man, then one of the girls would go along and sing to him, and sit on his knee and chat him up. Champagne was provided too, if they wanted it. Everybody enjoyed it. It really made the party go. Not just ordinary people, but all sorts of celebrities, TV stars, singers and entertainers, got the treatment.

When Christine told me about the Dial-a-Cake scheme I thought it sounded a smashing idea. I was working at the Festival Theatre at the time, but looking around for something different. I wanted to get more practice with cake decoration and frankly, I knew I could do a better job than they were doing. So I asked if they'd like to take me on. They suggested I should go back in a fortnight's time for a trial period, and they gave me ten 'torten' to decorate, all different shapes and sizes, all with some sort of message on. The working conditions were terrible. There wasn't even any hot water. So at first I said no, I didn't fancy it. But then we talked and I laid down my own conditions and insisted that I should be my own boss and do what I wanted. To my astonishment they agreed. So I stayed.

There were a lot of satisfactions in the job. When I went to work in the morning I knew that every day would be different. I could guarantee that I'd do about twenty cakes, but no two would be the same. If anyone asked for something very unusual I'd have to belt down to the supermarket and shop around. And it was all go, all excitement, because people were always in a rush. It was never 'Can you make a cake for my boss for next month, please?', always 'Look, sport, it's urgent! Half an hour, say?'

In some ways the business was successful and well run. We were usually busy. The advertising was effective. The girls used to dish out book-matches and bookmarks when they did a delivery, and we had our name on kitchen calendars, in ads in the local papers and in the Yellow Pages. We had two vans we used with 'Dial-a-Cake' blazoned over the sides, and they used to be seen dashing about all over the city, so I reckon everybody knew about us.

I think we got our charges right. The sponges actually cost about £2, but then we had to add our labour and overheads, and we charged from about £16 for an eight-inch Black Forest gateau, say, up to £30, depending on the size of the cake and the distance of the delivery. We tried to function within a five-mile radius if possible. The girls in the fish-net tights and the mandolin man were paid between £2.50 and £5.00 for each delivery, according to the distance. Christine and Peter each took about £150 a week out of the business, and I was paid nearly as much. But in the end we ran into difficulties for a combination of reasons. The flow of work was erratic. Some weeks there wasn't enough business, others there was so much that we couldn't keep up and, of course, you have to be reliable. You can't let people down on their big day. But basically the trouble was that it was run by a business man who couldn't do the cakes himself so he had to spend good money employing someone like me to do them for him, and it just wasn't cost-effective.

Nevertheless, I don't see why a scheme of this sort, if it's properly thought out, shouldn't take off in this country. It's something new and special, and it doesn't need a huge outlay of

capital to get started – just a 'phone and a van. You probably need
to set up in a place with a population of about 30,000 if you're
going to get enough work, and it needs to be a reasonably well-
heeled population. You need an organiser, like Christine, who's
good on the telephone and can sell the service and the product,
and has the knack of writing songs to order. It is just a knack; she
could do them standing on her head! You need someone to decorate the cakes, perhaps bake them too, but that's not necessary if
you have a good supplier close by. And you need a team of
young, good-looking freelance delivery boys and girls who look
great in a sexy uniform, can put on a performance and sing
reasonably well. There must be lots of students and actors who'd
be great. There's nothing to it really. Yes, I can't see any reason
at all why it shouldn't take off here. In fact, one of these days,
after I've done my 'Advanced Bread', I might well have a go
myself!

Val Bowes 'Flying Saucers'

I originally did a three-year training course at the North London
Polytechnic in Hotel Catering and Institutional Management, a
very thorough grounding in all forms of catering. The branch
I'm involved in now, providing food for pop and rock groups and
their back-up teams while they're on tour, is quite a recent
innovation. I suppose it began about six years ago when people
realised that there was a need for cooks to travel with the
musicians and their technical crews. Before that they'd had to
make do with the facilities provided by hotels and restaurants,
but that gave rise to all sorts of difficulties because rock groups
work such unsociable hours that they can throw an hotel into
chaos. When they have their own people to feed them, where and
when they need a meal, it makes their life a lot simpler. At first I
worked for a friend with his own catering company, but after a
while I decided I wanted to be on my own and do my own
organising. Do it my way. So I went solo about two years ago.

It's important to have the right name, and I'm very happy with
'Flying Saucers'. It ties in nicely with our motto which is 'Food
on the Move', and it's a bit of a pun, a joke. People remember it.

It wasn't my idea in the first place. It was suggested by an elderly friend of mine. He'd seen a roadside café called 'Flying Saucers' years and years ago, and remembered it ever since because he thought it was so appropriate. You need a good name, and you need contacts. Once you're known there's no difficulty in getting work. I've never advertised, but all the promoters and managers know about me, and my reputation has been built up by word of mouth. In this business you stand or fall on your own merits.

I've worked with dozens of groups, lots of big names: Adam and the Ants, Genesis, The Police, Roxy Music, Graham Parker – that's just a few, off the top of my head. I've travelled with them all over the place, in Europe as well as England. Tours often last between three and six weeks, whether we're in this country or abroad, but I occasionally do one-night gigs too, in venues like the Dominion in Tottenham Court Road or the Hammersmith Palais.

The set-up is always more or less the same. When we reach the venue we'll find that one room, or occasionally two, has been allocated for catering. It may have a supply of electricity and water laid on, but that's about all. Absolutely basic requirements. Sometimes not even electricity. So I have to supply everything I'm going to need. That room becomes 'home' for the day. That's where we cook and eat as a rule.

I take all my equipment with me. Sometimes I'll drive a transit van, which we hire, but at other times my stuff will go with the rest of the band's gear, and I prefer that. It all packs into four big metal boxes, flight boxes. One takes my Calor gas cooker. I need that most of all so that I can cook anywhere. The second box has cutlery and crockery, proper china crockery. I like things to look good and feel right. The third has pots and pans. The fourth, basic kitchen stores, a sort of buffer supply to keep us going until I manage to do some shopping – cereals, sugar, coffee, butter, that sort of thing. I also take lots of electrical adaptors, especially when we go abroad, so that if there is electricity I can use it, no matter what sort of differences there are in the plugs.

Although the set-up may sound primitive and makeshift, I've learned to be resourceful and adaptable, and there's absolutely nothing primitive and makeshift about my catering. I provide four good meals a day. We usually have an 8am 'get-in' (that's when we arrive at the venue and move in all the equipment) and I get down to work straight away and start with a good breakfast, cereals and fruit juice followed by bacon, eggs, sausages, tomatoes, that sort of thing, and coffee and toast. Then I do a buffet lunch, perhaps meat or fish with various salads. Before the show, when most of the preparation is finished, we'll have a good three-course meal. That will be at about six or seven o'clock. We'll start with proper homemade soup, then have a homemade meat course with three vegetables, and finish with a choice of puddings. Then, after the show, when the pressure's off at last and people can relax, I give them a buffet supper. Despite the three-course meal earlier on, they've used up so much energy by then that they're really hungry again.

Besides all this, I make up picnic boxes for the bus when we're on the move, and flasks for the drivers. I also provide all the drink that's required. If we're going abroad it's often cheaper to buy that on tour but some of the groups have special tastes so occasionally I have to do my buying in London before we leave. For instance, Genesis's special tipple is saké. I always have to take that with me because here I know exactly where to go to buy it.

It may sound like a glamorous life, but it's not. It's fun and it's exciting, but it's also hard work and very tiring. I usually start at 8 o'clock in the morning and work through solidly till midnight. And then, off we go to the next place. If I'm lucky I might have a proper bed in an hotel for the night, but I may have to put up with a sleeper coach if we're in a hurry to move on. So it's not a job for anyone who isn't young and fit. I should imagine it's a relatively short working life. Five years might be enough. After that you probably wouldn't be able to keep up with the physical demands of the work and would have to move into another form of catering. But I haven't really looked ahead as far as that.

One of the things about my business is that I often find myself organising several tours at the same time. For instance, I've catered for Roxy Music, Hot Chocolate and Genesis when they were all out on separate tours. I manage to cope because I have complete faith in the people working for me. I have a marvellous assistant, Judy Kelly, who is a close friend, adviser – well, it's difficult to describe her role. She's more than a PA. She can do virtually anything that needs doing and I really couldn't manage without her, whether she's in London, organising things from our office at Hammersmith or out on the road.

Besides Judy, I have a whole team of highly competent people, men and women, I can call upon to help me at any time. The number I need varies from three to twelve, depending on how much work I have on. They're all self-employed and very flexible. All of them have been on tour with me at some time or another and know how I like things done. I trust them totally to do the job properly. For instance, I always have flowers on the table for the evening meal. And I get the group the newspapers they want. Sometimes I buy sweets for them. It's these little extras that make the service I provide special. I set very high standards, and my staff keeps them.

The size of my catering team depends upon the size of the group and their crew. A couple of us can look after up to twenty people. If there are thirty, I have to make sure there are three of us, and four of us go out if there are more than that. But four is always the maximum because there just isn't room for more than four to work effectively in the sort of cooking space we have to use. It's not as if it's a grand hotel kitchen.

From our point of view, as far as the catering is concerned, the success of a tour depends upon masses of preparation beforehand. We need to be really well organised, have all our equipment ready and in tip-top order. For instance, at the moment we have a Genesis tour coming up in Europe. It'll last two weeks, and there'll be nine gigs, in different countries – Switzerland, France, Germany, Scandinavia and Belgium – and forty people will have to be fed four times a day. You just can't take off on a project like that without knowing exactly what you're doing and who's doing what. So the sooner a booking comes in, the better for us. We like to have two or three months' notice if possible. September to December, in particular, are very busy months in the pop world so they must be booked early. All the same, we try to be flexible and not disappoint people. Sometimes we do an English tour with a group, and then they say 'Look, we're going abroad next month and we just won't go without you to look after us.' That's very flattering, and we always try to reorganise ourselves to fit them in, but it's not always easy.

When we're on tour abroad the most difficult thing is probably the shopping, juggling the foreign money, trying to remember which currency we're using, working out values. I speak a couple of foreign languages, French and German, but all the same a lot of the marketing is done in sign language. It's often very funny. And I have to buy vast quantities of food, of course. Sometimes I might spend two or three hours in a supermarket in the morning, and I can fill up to six trolleys! Costing the whole project is very important – living within my budget and yet still keeping the food top quality. It has to be good, but it also has to make sense economically.

Although it's hard work, and I'm always up against the pressure of time, working against the clock, against the calendar, I enjoy it. It's a challenge. There's always something different happening. Sometimes quite exciting. Once when we were in Berlin we were caught up in a riot. A demonstration about nuclear warheads, I think. It was really quite frightening – crowds, tear gas, hundreds of police all over the place. But apart from things like that I enjoy the atmosphere. The guys we look after are always so appreciative. They treat me like mum. Tell me all their problems. And I've never worked with a bunch who weren't amiable, friendly, really nice. I like their music too. I enjoy listening to it while I'm working.

There's no doubt about it, though. The main satisfaction comes from doing the job well. It's creative. Let's face it, anybody can slap food on to a plate and say 'Get that inside you. That'll fill you up.' But what I do is much more than that. I create good meals out of raw materials. I make them taste good and look good, against all the odds of cooking conditions that can often be pretty primitive. It's like being a potter or a painter, except that you get instant feedback from the appreciation and pleasure of the people who are enjoying what you have created. I make a reasonable living out of my work. My accountant isn't complaining, not so far anyway. But no one goes into catering for the money, not if they have any sense. The reward lies in the personal satisfaction.

Elizabeth of 'Elizabeth and Paula'
Market Stallholders

It all began when British Rail closed down the old car park at our little railway station and opened a new de luxe one with special barriers and a pay kiosk. The old car park just sat there, unused and unlovely. It seemed such a waste. Then one of my friends in the village – she's an extraordinarily enterprising woman, a real ball of fire, used to sell her own ice-cream from a second-hand ice-cream van! – well, she got the idea that we could make it into a market. Good for the village people who could sell things they made or grew there, and good for the village as a whole too because it would bring in visitors, tourists, extra shoppers and business.

She spent a whole year badgering British Rail to give permission to use the car park once a month for a market, and at last she got it, and pays them a nominal fee for the privilege. Then she spent another year getting planning permission, organising insurance, looking into the legal side of things. One problem she came up against was that one of the local shopkeepers got up a petition to stop the market happening because he thought it would be bad for local traders. That petered out pretty quickly, though, because it soon became obvious that we weren't competing at all. The stuff we sold was quite different.

Anyway, she eventually got the project off the ground in April 1982. She decided the market would be open on the third Saturday of every month from April till October. It's out of doors, you see, so not much fun in the depths of winter. She charges us £5 a day, and we take our own tables and set them up. There's room for six stalls, but we book them from market to market and don't have to sign on for the whole season. Some stallholders change from month to month, which is good. It means there's always some variety, always something different to interest the shoppers. Paula and I have had a stall every time so far. We wouldn't do it if it rained but, in fact, every one of our Saturdays has been fine. There are all sorts of goods for sale – bric-à-brac, jumble, plants and garden produce, batik clothes, books, spare parts for cars, and Cancer Research takes a stall for publicity too.

Our stall sells fresh, homemade food. Cakes of all sorts,

including flapjacks, scones, biscuits, shortbread, rock buns, chocolate crunch and date cookies. Flapjacks are a special favourite, but all the stuff sells well – like, well, like hot cakes! My speciality is savoury flans. I'm well known for them in the village. I used to have savoury flan parties which were a bit of a joke, but I love making them and people are obviously more than happy to pay for them. A lot of our customers say 'The stuff is fresh, isn't it? Not out of the freezer?', and then they know they can take them home and put them safely into their freezers until they're needed. Often they ask me if I take orders for my flans, and I would happily do this, cook for people's freezers, though I know the money isn't all that good. Certainly you couldn't make a living out of our sort of cooking. But I'm always astonished at what people are prepared to pay for homemade food. For instance, I make a rather good Victoria sandwich cake, butter icing in the middle and on the top, and I can easily get £1.75 for that. Yet it's so quick and easy to make. I never can work out why people just don't get on with it and do their own baking, but obviously a lot of them would rather buy ours because we're nearly always sold out by midday.

So far our costing has been a bit haphazard. We're very new to the business, you see. At first we'd sell a rock cake for about 4p and people would say, 'You're mad! You could do much better than that.' Eventually we decided to sell them for about 10p each, and they still went. I suppose now we aim to get a price which is double the cost of our ingredients and packaging. We put flans into foil cases, for example, and the cakes go on pretty cardboard plates with doilies. Then everything, but everything, is wrapped up in cling film for hygiene's sake. So we make sure that all those bits and pieces are included in the basic cost we arrive at. What isn't included are the hours of work we put in. For instance, I'm a great shopper. I love it. I spend hours wandering around the shops looking for good bargains. I'll walk miles to save a few pence, though I know it's silly really. If I'm in a supermarket and see a really good large pack of streaky bacon at a bargain price I'll take it home and freeze it. And I go to the local garden centre for 5lb baskets of mushrooms. I find it's usually cheaper to buy in bulk, so I do that whenever possible, whenever the quality and price are right.

As well as my shopping time, I spend about four halfdays cooking for the morning of the market, so all in all, if I worked it out, I'd probably find I was getting paid a pittance for my time and labour. At the end of the market I might take home about £30, and though I know only half of that is really profit, I manage to buy the ingredients for my cooking from my housekeeping money without even noticing, so I always feel that it's all profit. I'm putting the money aside for my daughter's wedding, which isn't far in the future.

One of the real satisfactions of doing the cooking is the fact that people are actually prepared to pay good money for something you have made. And that they come back a month later and say 'I did enjoy the cakes and flans I bought last time. Please can I have the same again?' That really makes you feel good.

Both Paula and I are really very interested in food. Sometimes we go to Winkfield, which is the country base of the Cordon Bleu cookery school, for a day course. They're open to anyone who wants to go, and they're really helpful. We pick up lots of tips. They run weekly courses too, but we've never been on one of those. I believe you can find these cookery courses all over the country, and they're well worth investigating.

I like presenting food well too, making it look pretty. I always decorate the tops of the flans with patterns made from the ingredients themselves, tomato rings, sliced eggs, prawns nicely arranged, that sort of thing. And all the cakes are iced. Colour is very important. We try to make the whole layout bright and attractive, spread out on a snowy white cloth.

The other satisfaction, besides the food and the pocket money, is just the people, I suppose. I enjoy people. Sometimes they make me laugh, the funny things they say. One woman asked me exactly how many prawns I'd put into a prawn flan, as if I'd have time to count them! I think she thought the only ones were the ones I'd put on the top as a garnish. She didn't buy it anyway.

At present our market stall is just a very pleasant hobby. The cooking is easy, but satisfying. We have thought about doing more elaborate things but so far we haven't got around to it, mainly because our customers seem so happy with what we're providing at present, and it all goes so very well. We don't want to get too busy, too bogged down. It's just that we used to bake for our families and now they've left home, so we bake for the market instead. It's just a bit of fun really. We don't want it to become a burden, but we really do enjoy it.

Jenny Lindsay   School Lunchboxes

My way of cooking for cash probably seems very trivial to you, but it gives me a bit of extra money, which I need, and I enjoy it. I prepare picnic school lunches for an average of twelve children, but that's counting two of my own, every day of the week throughout the school year.

I charge 50p for each lunch and of that about 10p is profit, more or less, according to the season, because at some times of the year I can use masses of stuff out of my garden. People think I'm crazy, going to so much time and trouble for such a small amount of money. In fact, I don't look at it that way at all. I used to think I was crazy going to so much time and trouble just for my kids. You try preparing twelve school lunchboxes instead of two and you'll find it certainly doesn't take you six times as long, nor is it costing you six times as much. You can buy and cook in bulk, which is cheaper and, if you're well organised, there's less wastage. Anyway, I just enjoy feeding a lot of children. I keep saying to my husband 'We really should have a big family, you know,' but he just says, 'You're a crazy lady – we can hardly afford the two we've got.'

So, every morning I pack up these twelve picnic boxes. I love working out what I'm going to put in them. I make everything on a small scale, everything quite tiny. The kids love that. They'd rather have lots of little things than just a few big ones. I make my own yoghurt, and I often include some of that, flavoured either with homemade jam or crushed fruit from the garden. It's been raspberries, raspberries all the way this year. Then I do one or two little cubes of cheese. I buy big blocks from the cool counter of the freezer centre for as little as 89p a pound, cut it up into little chunks straight away and freeze it like that. It thaws very quickly. Sometimes I cook tiny little cocktail sausages and put them in as they are, or I make minute sausage rolls or patties. I don't have to worry about fuel costs for baking because I always have my Aga going. Sometimes I buy those miniature Hovis rolls and slice them up and butter them. Or I might include the tiny savoury biscuits you have with drinks sometimes. Small cartons of savoury salad or fruit salad go down well too, and sometimes chilled cucumber soup in the summer.

If I see anything special that's a bargain offer at the Cash and Carry – chocolate fingers, maybe, they're a favourite – I snap it up there and then. And I'm a great biscuit-maker. I bake masses and masses of biscuits, all different shapes, tastes and textures, often crunchy wholefood cookies, to make them chew properly. They're very cheap to make and the children adore them. I've got great tins of them, stacked away all over the house. And then, if they've all been very good, or the weather's rotten or they're having tests at school, I might slip in a little block of chocolate, or two or three jelly babies in a little twist of tissue paper, as a special treat. But only if they have an apple too because that'll clean their teeth. I know how worried mothers get about sweets and tooth decay these days. I worry too – I don't want my children to have any more fillings than are absolutely necessary.

I'm very conscious of health and nutrition, and I try to make sure that whatever goes into the picnic box adds up to a well-balanced meal. I try to work out that there's protein, calcium, plenty of vitamins and fibre. There's always a little fruit, perhaps a tangerine or a few nuts and raisins, never too much sugary or starchy stuff. It's not only their teeth I worry about; I don't want them to get fat or spotty either or lack energy. I suppose I'm a bit of a fusspot, but I do like to see kids positively shining with health. And you see, I know a lot of other mothers, who either can't afford school dinners or whose children won't eat them, feel just the same as me but haven't got the time, the facilities or the imagination to fiddle about the way I do. If you're doing a full-time job, and then you've got your cooking and housework to do when you get home from work, you're not going to spend your time making little patties the size of a 50p piece are you? But me – I love it! I make minute little sandwiches too, chop the crusts off and then cut them into all sorts of shapes. I know people say 'Oh, sandwiches – boring!' but children love sandwiches, especially if the bread's thin and the filling is tasty. The old favourite, egg, tomato and mayonnaise all mashed up together, is one of their top ten, but they like mashed banana too and peanut butter and jam (yes, really, one spread thickly on top of the other), and all kinds of meat and fish pastes and pâtés. I make a lot of pâtés myself, just so that I can be quite sure the ingredients are good, and also because it's much cheaper that way if you've got a few tasty economical recipes. I do lovely kipper and mackerel pâtés, and I do a smashing pâté de campagne made from sausage meat. I cut the recipe out of a newspaper years ago and I've used it ever since. It's just about disintegrating now, all stuck together with sticky tape.

So there I am every morning, filling my twelve picnic boxes, making them look as pretty as possible. I do think food has to be colourful and attractive so that children can't resist the look of it, quite apart from the smell and taste. Fortunately I don't have to include a drink because they've got a drinks vending machine at school, and they don't need knives and forks because nearly everything I put in is finger food, though they have to have spoons, of course, if it's a yoghurt day. I've got a large supply of plastic ones. I also buy vast quantities of paper napkins because children can be messy little creatures, especially when they're feeling silly, and want to let off steam.

When the boxes are filled, I pile them all in the boot of the car and drive them, and my own two children, to school. I unload at the school gates, pile up the boxes and wait until their owners collect them. That's the theory, at any rate. In fact the children are usually all there waiting for me, and they hurl themselves at the boot as I grind to a halt, yelling 'What've we got today? What've we got today?' They keep me on my toes, you see. I have to keep the standards very high, and the ideas flowing, or they'd be the first to tell me off. Fortunately I haven't had any complaints yet!

When I drive back to collect the children, I park the car, open up the boot and the boxes are flung in with gay abandon, ready for tomorrow's feast. As soon as I get home I open them up, remove the debris, check up to see if anything's been left – because if there are a lot of leftovers that's a sure sign that what I thought was a bright new idea has turned out to be a bummer – do any washing up that's necessary, wipe out the boxes and leave them standing on the sideboard to be filled up next morning. I'll have worked out during the day what I'm going to put in, and I'll have done nearly all the cooking or preparation by then, because I like to spend the evenings with the family, or out in the garden, not stuck in the kitchen.

All that remains is to collect the money. On Friday mornings every child hands over his £2.50. If he doesn't bring the money, there's no Friday lunch for him so I always get paid. It's a foolproof method. One Friday one little boy forgot his money and I said, very sternly 'Sorry, no money, no food.' Actually, I fully intended to give it to him anyway, but before I knew what he was doing he had rushed into school, asked a teacher to telephone his mum because it was an emergency, and had the poor woman cycling frantically along the street, still half-dressed. The teacher was not very pleased when she discovered the nature of the 'emergency', but his mother was abject, begged me to not to cross him off my school lunchbox list and promised it would never happen again. It was all very embarrassing. I kept apologising too, but the fact remains that since then I've never had any trouble on 'collecting day' at all.

Okay, so there are easier ways of making £5 a week or whatever. All I know is that I like doing it. I love pleasing the children. I know I'm using my garden, my Aga and my deep freeze very economically. The project makes me organise my time so that I make the most of every minute. And I've learned to shop sensibly, buy in bulk and watch for bargains, which means that my housekeeping stretches much further too, so I call that a hidden earning. I also know that on £5 a week, if I'm sensible and do some of my own dressmaking, I can dress myself very nicely, thank you, without having to dip into my husband's pay packet and worry about taking money that should be put aside for the rates or the gas bill. So I'm not complaining. And neither are my pint-sized customers!

Isobel Dinton   'Country Fare'

I found myself sharing in the running of a small village café almost by chance. There'd been a café in our village for years but it had gone steadily downhill until it was all juke boxes, fruit machines and hell's angels. An absolute headache for the people in the village, especially the ones who lived next door to it. Even the parish council had discussed what they could do about it but hadn't managed to come up with any bright ideas. Fortunately it went out of business and closed down, so three of us, all married women in our forties with teenage children, decided to see if we could make a go of it. None of us had any experience really, except that I used to take a caravan to agricultural shows and fairs and sell tea and buns to the visitors, and one of the others had done a bit of hotel work and served in a cake shop as vacation jobs during her student days.

The business side was a bit complicated because a commercial group had bought a fourteen-year lease on the property from the owners, and there were ten years of the lease still remaining, and it was those ten years that were for sale. The building was pretty primitive, just a hut really, but well situated in the centre of the village, with a good-sized garden outside so that people could sit out there in the summer. We thought that might appeal to holiday-makers. And we had the idea of selling locally made crafts as a sideline. There was plenty of parking space nearby and we knew that was very important. People could easily stop if they saw our board and fancied popping in. We talked the matter over with a friendly solicitor, and at first he said, 'Oh no, I don't think it's a money-making venture really.' Then he went on holiday himself and saw other little cafés and gift shops just like the one we'd been describing, and suddenly he became very enthusiastic – just when we'd begun to go off the idea! Anyway, he rang up the leaseholder and there was a whole lot of bargaining and making offers and being turned down and starting again, until in the end we got the lease, and the contents – tables, chairs, floor-covering, an old cooker and some cupboards – for a very fair price. We still had to pay rent to the owners, of course, and rates, but since we were doing it primarily as a hobby, to start with at any rate, and as an amenity for the village, and didn't really need to make money out of it, we thought we could attract enough business to cover our costs and leave a little over to pay ourselves expenses.

We didn't need to borrow a penny from the bank. We were able to scrape up enough ourselves to buy the lease, pay the first quarter's rent and acquire extra equipment like cutlery and china and rush matting. We made pretty curtains and tablecloths from material we bought in the market, and decorated the place ourselves. Our colour scheme was ivory, burnt orange and brown, and it looked very fresh and country-ish. Our husbands helped us to make pale, stripped shelving from bits and pieces of timber they picked up for a song, and sorted out the electrics for us. There was no piped gas in the village so we cooked by Calor gas.

Most of the crafts we sold we managed to get from local people on a sale or return basis, so that didn't take a lot of capital, though we did buy some beautiful handmade candles, I remember, and some pottery. There were a few extras, like stationery, wrapping paper, installing a phone, a bit of advertising, but it didn't amount to much. Oh, and a fridge. We got one for £10 from the small ads in the local paper and it gave us good service for eight years. We whipped masses of things from our own kitchens – pots, pans and dishes, brushes and mops, flower vases. We always had flowers on the tables. Our husbands began to get quite peeved when they discovered yet another piece of equipment had gone missing!

We opened in June 1974 with a gala opening. The local supermarket manager, who was also chairman of the parish council, came and cut a ribbon across the doorway, and had the first cup of coffee on the house. We wanted his good will because we reckoned he'd recommend us to his customers, which he did. We were a mutual benefit society really because we bought quite a lot of our provisions from his shop.

To start with we did pretty well, better than we expected in fact. We closed on Mondays, and divided the Tuesdays to Saturdays into halfday sessions. Since there were three of us it meant that one did four halfdays one week in three, while the other two did three halfdays, and whoever was on in the morning overlapped the lunch hour with whoever was doing the afternoon duty. We tended to settle into a routine. I used always to do Tuesday afternoon and Thursday morning, then we'd work out Fridays and Saturdays from week to week to fit in with our family commitments. We had a rather complicated roster system which was very flexible. We could always swop around with each other if we needed to for any reason, but it was good to have regular times because then you got regular customers, and that was one of the nicest things about it, making real friends among the customers, people from all walks of life – lorry drivers, teachers, retired people, reps, even gypsies. They were amazing, the gypsies, very honest. And the old lady, the matriarch, kept the children on a very tight rein. They had to behave, and were much more disciplined than the children of some of the trendy, middle-class mums we had. Their children would have demolished the entire place if we'd let them get away with it.

Even when we weren't on duty, there was still work to do. We took it in turns to do the cleaning on Mondays, so that was one Monday in three, for at least two or three hours. Then each one of us had a special responsibility. I was in charge of organising and buying the food and planning the menus. I used to go to the Cash and Carry most Mondays, and there was a splendid man who brought us home-cured hams. I was on good terms with the village greengrocer too, and he always did well by us. Diane was the craft lady, buying stock, pricing up, arranging the shelves artistically. Jane was in charge of the books, writing letters paying bills, banking, doing orders and invoices, seeing the VAT man and the accountant. But we all had a say in everything really, and we all kept an eye on what the others were doing. If they didn't like my menus or thought I was paying too much for butter, they'd tell me. If we didn't like the crafts, we'd say so. We only wanted to sell things, either food or gifts, that we ourselves would be happy to buy. We always kept that as our guiding rule. The three of us had to agree on standards, using our own personal taste as a guideline. At our staff meetings, once a month, on Mondays, we had some pretty hefty arguments but we usually made sure we reached agreement by the time we'd finished, no matter how long it took us.

As well as all this, we made nearly all the food ourselves in our own kitchens. Whoever was on for lunch used to bring in the lunch for the day. Usually she'd cook it the day before, then warm it through in the café because the cooker was pretty dreadful, though eventually we did manage to buy two splendid new ones, when the business had a little boom. We all made sponge cakes and scones too. When we started we intended to have light lunches, quiches and salads, homemade soup and sandwiches, ice-cream and gateaux for afters. But we had to change that because we got a lot of lorry drivers who wanted something more substantial, so we began to add stews and casseroles and meat pies to our repertoire. Then we got busier and had to have an assistant, a woman from the village who had helped out at the local pub but wanted to join us. She came in for two or three hours a day to help with the lunches, and occasionally do a halfday stint.

We really got a lot of customers. We were near the village primary school so every afternoon all the young mums congregated in the café for a chat before they picked up their children. The place absolutely hummed with their talk and laughter – great fun! And we were near the bus stop and the launderette so a lot of people who'd been in the village to shop or do their washing, and found themselves with time on their hands, used to come in for half an hour or so. A lot of folks who were old or lonely came in just for company, and we always made sure we had time to talk to them. Sometimes we'd manage to sit down and have a cup of tea with them, which they always seemed to appreciate. Then during the summer we had holiday-makers. We were the only place serving afternoon tea for miles around, so we were frantically busy, from 3.30 till 5.30pm say, all through July and August. I remember one day, at half past five, putting up the 'closed' sign on the door, and a man actually climbed in through the window! 'Tea!' he moaned. 'Tea, for the love of Allah.' How could I refuse him?

We were very busy during the summer, and for the two months before Christmas. People came in to buy cards and presents, but usually stayed for coffee and cake too. But business was very slack for the first three months of the year or so. We had to have enough money in the bank to see us through till Easter really, and we did occasionally have cash flow difficulties when we knew we couldn't pay a bill till we had a little bit more money in hand. But we just juggled things around a bit and got by. We never needed to borrow from the bank; we were always determined not to do that. We were very careful with our buying and spending and always had a contingency fund on deposit in case of financial disasters. I think we only had to dip into it once, when we needed an expensive piece of equipment, a new food mixer I believe. We had the occasional nasty experience. Three times, in very close succession, we were burgled, but fortunately we were covered by insurance, so that was more of a nuisance than a major drama. Then we thought we'd got a contract to provide twenty-five lunches a day for a new factory that opened on the little trading estate in the village. That regular income would have given us real stability and we'd have been able to expand, but the whole thing fell through in the end. The manager decided it would be better to employ his own kitchen staff and serve coffee and rolls in the rest room on the premises. That was a great blow, a real disaster.

In the end, gradually, the business became more difficult, and we found it more and more of a struggle. There were lots of reasons for this. To begin with, we had a rent reappraisal after our third year, and again after our seventh, and by that time the rent had doubled. Secondly, the rates doubled. Unfortunately, our customers didn't double. And all our other overheads shot up – telephone, electricity, gas. It also cost more to buy the ingredients for our food, and it's all very well saying 'Charge more', but we knew that our customers were feeling the pinch too, and just couldn't afford to spend more. So, instead of coming in and having a cup of coffee and two ham rolls, they began to buy a cup of tea and a couple of biscuits. What with the recession and widespread unemployment, we couldn't hope to win. But the last straw came from the environmental health officer. He suddenly announced we had to have hand basins with hot and cold water installed in our two loos. Always before that we'd let customers use the hand basin in the kitchen, and gave them scented soap and nice clean towels. We could see his point of view. He had to enforce his rules, I suppose. On the other hand, we were just breaking even, we only had eighteen months of our lease left and the new plumbing would have cost us a fortune and got us into debt. So we decided to close down, and handed the rest of the lease back to the owner. The café is just standing empty now, and it's a great shame. I keep meeting old customers and they all say how much they miss it. One of them has actually had a nervous breakdown, and I can't help feeling it was perhaps her daily visit to us for a cup of tea and a little chat that managed to keep her going.

The eight years we ran our business were very hard work and we didn't make much money, just pocket money really. But I don't regret any of it. Funny things happened. Like the time we got the wrong pie out of the fridge and served minced steak and onions with custard! And one day a little shrew wandered in and we had all these great burly lorry drivers chasing it around with brushes and brooms, trying to get it outside but absolutely terrified they might hurt it. We used to do a wonderful Christmas dinner too, starting with a glass of sherry on the house, and keeping the price as low as we possibly could. All our regular customers came and it was just like a real party. A family party. We even wore paper hats! That was what made it all so worth while, the gentle, day-by-day friendship between us and our customers. They were all so pleasant, they'd even lend a hand with clearing the tables and washing up if they saw we were pushed, or rush over to the supermarket to buy extra butter and ham for sandwiches if we were very busy and running out of food. They'd dry dishes for us, carry trays, bring us flowers from their gardens for the tables, do all sorts of odd jobs, then actually pay their bills and thank us! People can be very kind, and I do miss them.

Lynn Verity   Cooking Co-operative

Ever since I moved to this town I've felt happy and at home in the arts centre. I brought my children here for workshops and other activities, and occasionally I'd stay on to lend a hand. I really liked the place, and it was particularly convenient since we live just round the corner. I had eaten in the restaurant here and loved the food and, you know, even now when I'm one of the cooks, I'd still rather eat here than anywhere else.

The cooking began purely by chance. I used to help out at a playgroup and one of the other mums asked whether I'd like to come along to the arts centre to help serve at lunchtime when they were busy. At that time I had no thought of cooking. I'd always been interested in nutrition, but not so much in cooking. I had no training at all, though I was always trying out new dishes at home. At first I came along on two occasions just really to watch and see how they organised themselves. Then I went along to a cooks' meeting and they asked me if I'd like to stand in as an extra server if one of the group had to be away. It was a busy time just then, our local festival was in progress and they needed eight cooks, two servers and a washing-up lady.

As a server I earned 10 per cent of the total takings for the day, with a guarantee that it shouldn't be less than £5. If it was a bad day and 10 per cent didn't amount to £5, it was made up to that figure from a reserve fund. On a busy day they could take £100, so you could go home with £10 in your pocket. There were a few perks too, like leftover food that I was given to take home for my own family, and since the food is so good that was a real bonus.

One of our problems in the co-operative is that the food doesn't go on to the next day. Each cook has to take home whatever is left, and there's bound to be wastage. A lot of it can't be frozen, things like flans, cheesecake, egg mayonnaise, salads. It has to be eaten on the day, either by customers or by the cook's family, or be given away. Fortunately there's not often much left. If it's just stuff like a few biscuits or a chunk of cake it can go into the kids' packed lunches for school. But we can never tell how much we'll need. It's so embarrassing to run out of food halfway through the lunch period that a lot of us overcater, but that's very extravagant. Sometimes when we're expecting a quiet day we're busy and are frantic by 12.45 when all the soup's gone and we're getting low on quiches. Then the next week we'll think 'Ah! Last Friday was very busy. We'll be ready for the rush this Friday.' And nobody comes. You can't win.

At first I thought I'd never be able to be a cook for the co-operative. I thought I wouldn't be able to do the amount that was needed or keep up the standard the others had set. Then gradually I began to think 'I don't know, I might be able to do as well as that.' I started off with a one-off event on a Sunday afternoon, just cakes and biscuits. That was my first go. Then a friend of mine joined the co-operative and I decided to do a 'half-cook' with her, sharing it between us. That was always on a Monday which I hated because it meant I had to cook on a Sunday. My husband plays football on Saturday – it's his job – so really we had no weekend. But I didn't want to give up and I thought this was a way in. So I hung on, waiting for a better day to turn up.

Suddenly Wednesday became free. One of the women left the group for some reason or another, and I jumped into her place. So then I was the Wednesday cook, shopping and cooking on Tuesday, serving my food on Wednesday. Two full days a week. Well, no, that's an exaggeration, not two *full* days. I begin at 9am on both days, but I'm always finished by 3pm. Together, for the two days' work, I'd get my expenses back plus 30 per cent of the two days' takings. I have to pay out about £25 for the ingredients for one day's food. That's quite a lot the very first time, before you've made anything. A lot of women I know just can't lay their hands on £25 to invest in a day's cooking. They just haven't got £25 to spare. I was lucky to be able to get hold of it. Once you've started, the earnings are very useful if your husband's not making big money. All my cash goes straight into the housekeeping.

I get my recipes from all over the place. I spend a lot of time in the library looking at their cookery books, and others come from newspapers and magazines. I do quite a lot of my shopping in the market. Fortunately, in our town, that's held on Tuesday which is my shopping day anyway. The co-operative specialises in wholefood and vegetarian cookery, and there are two wholefood market stalls. The arts centre has an arrangement with them that, because we buy so much from them, we can get a 10 per cent discount. Also I can buy cheap cracked eggs in the market; they're marvellous for flans. Usually I get my vegetables and fruit there too, but I always check off the prices against the going rate in the supermarket because occasionally the supermarket is cheaper. We know we could save money by bulk buying, but we don't. The arts centre hasn't got much storage, and if we bought as a group and kept the food in our own homes it would be very time-consuming, going back and forth to one another's houses to get our own share weighed out and taken home. Sometimes it's more important to save time than money.

I've had to lay out a bit of money on equipment, mainly flan dishes and extra pots and pans, not a great deal though. I didn't need to borrow money. I only needed to get hold of that first £25 and then I was all right. I haven't come across many difficulties in working with the group. It depends upon your temperament, I suppose. I'm very easy-going by nature. Anyway, we only get together once a month. The girl I work with on Wednesdays, Jo, is as easy-going as I am so we get on very well together. In fact we've hit it off so well that the pair of us have done some outside catering together.

We did a supper party for a hundred for the rugby club. They paid £1.50 a head and we ended up with £50 each, so everyone was happy. We did chicken with salads and French bread, and served it through a hatch, so it wasn't really a lot of work for that sort of money. And we did the food for a conference in the centre, a whole day's food, coffee and biscuits at midmorning, flans, salads and puddings at lunchtime, then tea and cakes in the afternoon. There were 160 people to feed and only the two of us. The whole place was crammed because the restaurant was open too, but our catering was quite separate from the group's on that day. We did it ourselves and we took the profits. We planned it very well, but there was a lot of work to be got through beforehand and we worried ourselves sick – 160 people! But it was a great success. Every success adds to your self-confidence. I organised my brother's wedding reception a little while ago and that helped me to realise I could do it if I organised myself properly.

I used to do extra cooking for a vegetarian restaurant in the town too, flans and cakes, the same sort of thing I do for the co-operative. The owner used to come to my house one day to pick up the food she needed for the next, and she paid me twice the cost of my ingredients plus 10p per item for electricity. I gave it up in the end because it was too much of a good thing, but I think there's plenty of that sort of work going for people who want to do it, cook well and find it enjoyable. You don't earn a lot, but you don't take any risks either.

Personally, I prefer cooking as one of a group, though sometimes difficulties arise. Occasionally there's rivalry as to which cooks should do a special event which might bring in a good profit, like a craft market or a popular concert. We have to talk it out and try to take turns so that everybody who wants to gets a fair share of the extra work that's going. We suffer from lack of communication too. No matter how hard everybody tries, the centre can be rather chaotic and we're not always informed in advance about everything that's happening. But, despite that, I find so many satisfactions in my work that I hardly know where to begin my list. First of all, I love the planning and choosing the recipes, though I admit I hate the shopping and cooking when the kids are on holiday from school. I also love the presentation, making what I've done look good, so that people admire it when they come to the counter and try to decide what they're going to eat. Often everything looks so tempting that they take ages to make up their minds, and sometimes I begin to feel quite impatient, until I remember that it's a compliment really. And I love the whole business of being in the arts centre, the atmosphere of the restaurant. It always feels a nice, happy place to be. And you can bring the children in with you because there are other kids around all the time, so there's no problem of getting baby-sitters organised if they're off school. If they happen to be ill, or we go away for a week, someone will always stand in for you. It's quite different from an ordinary job where you get set leave.

I suppose the main joy is that the group is very friendly and supportive. Though we don't see each other often, we always know the others are there and will back us up if we need it. If someone's depressed, worried or going through a sticky patch in their marriage, anything at all, we know that the others are on our side, and care, and will do anything they can to help.

Jo Lamb   WI Market

I trained as a cook, years and years ago, at West Hampstead Domestic Science College. I did a one-year course, and we were taught everything, a very thorough grounding. I must have been cooking all my life off and on, for my family, of course, but mostly what you would call 'institutional cooking'. Before I was married I was a cook at Benenden School. Then I ran a factory canteen, moved on to Godolphin School for Girls, and several other jobs, all interspersed with having children, following my naval husband around the world whenever I could, and looking after a home and family. I spent twelve years cooking in a village school. That was wonderful, just like having a huge family. I've always enjoyed cooking for numbers rather than for small groups. It comes naturally to me.

I thought I'd given all that up, when suddenly I had a telephone call from a friend who was about to launch a WI market in a neighbouring village. She felt she needed a professional cook to be involved in the food side of the project, just to make sure the standards were kept up and to be able to advise the other less-experienced cooks if they ran into difficulties. I don't run it or anything. There is a food controller who is in charge of the food, and she receives it and checks it for quality and presentation. But I can stand in for her if necessary.

Pastry is my speciality. I make lots of savoury plate pies, about ten a week, steak and kidney, chicken, whatever I fancy. They always go, straight away, and I tend to have lots of steady orders for them which is very satisfying. But the good thing about cooking for the market is that really I can make anything that takes my fancy. I'm not tied. So, when the mood takes me, I make meringues, biscuits, sponge cakes, lemon meringue pies. I do special celebration cakes too, especially for Mother's Day and Christmas. I enjoy making them look lovely, presenting them well, and they're a great success.

I frequently try to do something a little bit different. It doesn't always work, but if it doesn't the family eats the rejects. Thursday evening there's always great excitement when the grandchildren come in to see what's going spare. Nothing ever gets wasted. Everything is eaten. Misshapen biscuits taste just as good as perfect ones, even if I can't offer them for sale. What I cook is also tied up with the season. People want different things at various times of the year. In the summer they're looking for ideas to go with their salads or into a picnic basket. In the winter they're more interested in buying the basics for a good, filling, hot meal.

Though I don't spend hours and hours working at it, it is a continuous interest and occupation because I enjoy thinking of what I'll make, then shopping around and looking for bargains. If I see something that is good value, I buy there and then and store it in my friend's deep freeze. The basic ingredients, that is, not the finished product, because that's against WI rules. They're very strict. I tend to buy my basics from a good quality supermarket. Meat I buy from the butchers in Butcher Row in our local market town. The best butchers are still to be found in

Butcher Row, which pleases me, an old tradition. I buy in reasonably large quantities, in packs of about 5lb. But I get my steak and kidney separately, not all mixed up together the way a lot of people buy them. I don't think you get the best quality by doing that, and we have to think of quality control all the time. Vegetables I often get from the WI market, so I make money there and plough some of it back for the benefit of other producers. That pleases me too.

I start preparing my pastry on a Wednesday. We're not allowed to start the cooking process more than two days before the selling day. So, on Wednesdays I work out a plan of what I'm going to do, and rub the fat into the flour. Then on Thursdays I cook, from about 8am till lunchtime. The tedious bit is the packaging. High standards are laid down for this, and they are a bit boring, though easy enough to keep to. Everything has to be wrapped and then labelled with my name and address, a description of the contents and the main ingredients. This is a safety precaution, I suppose, just in case of food poisoning or something like that. Then I'm at the market on Fridays, most Fridays, from 8.30am until midday.

Why do I do it? Not for the money, that's for sure. I only make about one-third profit on the price of my ingredients when I take everything into account, transport, time, fuel and so on. And you have to keep a very close watch on prices because they tend to change from week to week almost, so there has to be constant reassessment. It's a pleasant, sociable project, not a money-making concern. I do it because I like it. I like the actual time in the market especially. It's a very pleasant, friendly way of passing a morning. It also makes me get myself organised. I can't let things slip. I know I have to have all my other jobs, gardening, housework and so on, organised by Thursday, so it's a very good discipline.

Part of the pleasure of being part of an organisation like this is seeing what other people do. Some of them bring in excellent produce. The stalls sometimes look quite wonderful. I'm always full of admiration for other people's skills. Yes, that's important you see, being part of a friendly group which shares the same aims. And though it doesn't make much money, there's enough to buy something special occasionally, a really good saucepan or something. At present I'm aiming at a deep freeze of my own because so far I've had to share space in a neighbour's. It may take me about twenty years to save up enough money for one, but never mind, it's nice to have something to work towards.

Penny Pleasance   Cake Decorator

I went to the Hartley Smith School of Icing – thirty years ago! It doesn't exist now. I did evening classes there for a year. I saw it advertised in a national paper and thought it would be a good thing to do. My only regret is that I didn't bother to take my City and Guilds exam in cake icing. If I'd done that I would have been able to teach, you see, and that's really a very profitable way of using your skills. I'd advise anyone interested in cake icing to do their City and Guilds. Most colleges and polytechnics run courses these days, I believe. And there are several schools of cake icing all over the country.

I keep busy. I've always got something on the go. But it all comes in through reputation. I never advertise because I'm afraid I might get inundated with orders and I wouldn't want that. I make all sorts of cakes, for weddings and wedding anniversaries, birthdays, christenings, confirmations, Christmas. I've done cakes for children too, sponges usually, all different shapes – little houses, boats, trains with a string of carriages, decorated with smarties and tiny sweets. I use basic cake tins and cut the sponges into the right shape, and then the cake just builds itself up as I do it. It's like painting a picture. I start with just an idea and see where it leads me. At the other extreme I've just done one for an eightieth birthday. Then I had another interesting commission, a cake for the thirtieth birthday of the art group I belong to. I decorated that one with swans because our head-quarters are beside a river, very pretty, and a lot of us paint river scenes. Yes, I am an artist and I think that's very important because cake decorating is a bit like painting. The real satisfaction comes from actually doing it rather than the money. It's certainly an advantage to be able to draw. When I get an order for a cake I always find out what the person's particular interests are, and then make a special design and draw all the decorations which would be most appropriate. For instance, if it's for someone who likes tennis, I might make little tennis racquets. If it's for someone in the theatre, I'll do the masks of comedy and tragedy. For a christening I'll make a little cradle, with pillow and coverlet; or I might work out a musical motif, or tiny instruments, for a musician.

I make all the decorations myself – roses, birds, bells, fans. It needs tremendous patience. Sometimes I put a plaque in the centre, and prop it up with a tiny rose, and there'll be a message or greeting piped on it. All these decorations are made from pastilage, which is a sort of gum paste mixed with marzipan. It's marvellous for modelling, but you have to make loads of spares because they get broken so easily. At the corners of the cake I put 'run-outs', which are decorative shapes made from icing sugar. You trace the pattern on to waxed paper, pipe on a thick outline and then make icing sugar to a softer consistency to fill in the centre. Run-outs are immensely time-consuming to make but they give a very professional finish. If it's a wedding cake I sometimes line the underside of the run-out with a scrap of silk to match the colour of the wedding dress.

I don't use complicated nozzles and piping equipment; I just make simple icing bags from greaseproof paper. As well as the pastilage decorations I use other bits and pieces to give a pretty finish. For instance, I press maidenhair fern and put it on to birthday cakes; I grow the fern myself, in the garden. And I'm always collecting things that might come in useful. Sometimes I keep them for years and years before they're needed but they always get used in the end – decorative leaves, silver ribbons, scraps of satin, all sorts of things.

It takes me a very long time to make a cake, especially something like a three-tier wedding cake. I like to get the order at least three months before the day itself, that's the maturing time. I make the cake straight away, wrap it up in greaseproof paper and foil, and then put it away for a month and forget about it. The recipe is one I've put together myself, from my own experience. I always use the same one. After a month I get the cake out and add some brandy. I like brandy in a cake. Then a month before the wedding I put on a layer of marzipan and leave it for another week, and then I'm ready for the icing. A wedding cake needs three coats of icing, and you have to wait ten days after the last coat to put on the decoration. The decoration is done in the final ten days. The icing base must be firm but not too hard, otherwise it wouldn't cut. I suppose I spend about twenty-four hours in all decorating a three-tier cake, but it could be longer with a particularly intricate design.

I find there's one book that I use a lot to help me with ideas and techniques, Evelyn Wallace's *Cake Decorating and Sugarcraft* published by Hamlyn. It covers the sort of course I did at the Hartley Smith school. It's designed for housewives, students and teachers and is very thorough. I've used my copy continuously for ten years now, and I wouldn't be without it. Most libraries should have a copy.

People are prepared to pay quite a lot of money for a decorated cake, perhaps £25 for a single-tier one, £75 for a three-tier. I suppose some would go up to £100. But they are expensive to make. I should think the basic ingredients for a three-tier cake cost about £25, and that's before icing and everything, just the cake itself. Marzipan's a terrible price, and you have to pay for the board, the albumen, the icing sugar and all the little extras. So really, if you've put in twenty-four hours' work, you're not getting a huge return for your labour. But with something artistic you can't really price yourself by the hour; it's the satisfaction that matters. On the other hand, it doesn't pay to underprice yourself. People don't trust a cut-price job.

I do like the money it brings in, my own personal money. I like having that little bit of independence. But there are easier ways of earning it. Once I ran a little course in Christmas cake decoration for twelve women. The vicar's wife arranged it, and we used the vicarage kitchen. We had four two-hour sessions. Each woman brought her own cake and her own ingredients for the decorating. The first week I taught them to do the marzipan, the second week we put on the first coat of icing and made the decorations, the third week we put on another coat, and got a bit more advanced. And I threw in making pastilage roses as a little extra. Then the final week we did the actual finished decoration. It didn't cost me anything, and they all paid me a fee, even the vicar's wife though we were using her kitchen, so that was very profitable. And I loved doing it. I'd like to do that sort of thing again. When it was first suggested to me I said 'Oh no, I couldn't possibly!', but I had a go and I found I could. And they all said how much they'd enjoyed it, and they were so proud of their lovely cakes.

That's one of the troubles, of course. You take so many pains to make the thing look beautiful, there's a terrible feeling when it's cut up and the decoration goes. All the same, I do like to be there when it's first cut into, to see if it's really well matured. In fact, I feel terrified of the actual cutting. I always use the same recipe, the same cooker, the same temperature and timing, yet again and again the cake turns out quite different. I always think 'This time it'll have gone wrong.' I went to a christening the other day and they insisted that I had to do the cutting myself, and my hand was really shaking. But it was all right, thank heavens. In fact, touch wood, it's never let me down. Not yet!

Peter Combes 'Nadder Catering'

My business started eighteen months ago, almost by chance. My basic training was in the wine trade, but after three and a half years of that I decided I wanted some time off and went to Italy for six months. While I was there, a friend asked me to take on the job of reorganising a sort of holiday complex she owned, a complete village. It was beautiful, it was popular, but it was costing her money instead of making it. I spent a lot of time and thought on its problems, worked out what the basic costs were, then doubled them in charges to holiday-makers in order to pay for repairs, maintenance and so on. One had to be realistic. And it worked. I turned it into a paying concern.

I suppose that was my first taste of professional business organisation, and I revelled in it. But I was just twenty-three, and I felt that life was passing me by in that lovely remote Italian village. So, back I came to England and, after a little more experience in the wine trade in London, my itchy feet led me home to Wiltshire, where my family has lived for hundreds of years. I set up my own wine business, 'Nadder Wines', in 1977 as a wholesaler. Business flourished and, after I'd been going for a couple of years or so, a friend of mine got married and asked me to do the drinks. The catering was being done by yet another friend, Jenny. We worked together, and were able to watch each other's performance as it were. She liked my wines and I liked her food, and we both had the same sort of style, so we decided to work together as often as we could, on an unofficial basis. Not a partnership or anything like that, but we'd recommend each other for functions and join forces when possible. This worked splendidly for a while then suddenly she decided it was all getting too much for her and she'd have to sell out. I was devastated. I suddenly saw £30,000 of turnover disappearing down the drain. And 'Nadder Wines' wasn't as healthy as it had been because suddenly we were into hefty competition from the supermarkets and bargain wine shops that could undercut us easily. I had a ghastly Christmas wondering what on earth to do, when my sister suddenly said 'Why don't you and I buy the business between us?' She was used to large-scale cooking. She'd run a BBC canteen and done lots of other major catering jobs. We told Jenny we were interested and she was thrilled and sold it to us straight away without a second thought. We paid £10,000 for it, the good will and the equipment, having borrowed most of the money from the bank on a three-year loan. Then, on the very day I signed the contract and came rushing home waving it in triumph, my sister announced that she was pregnant and wouldn't be able to help me for long. Second disaster! However, we coped. One of my sister's great friends said she'd step into the breach.

We got 'Nadder Catering' off the ground in February with a huge drive to drum up customers, pestering everyone we knew, having a party to launch ourselves in style, telling the world who we were and what we were about. I'm a typical Taurus, a real bull in a china shop, but it's the only way I can work. It's only when I'm pushed right into a difficult situation that I can pull it off. I'm bored rigid by plain sailing. Business snowballed. People were extremely kind and gave us a lot of opportunities to show what we could do. Again and again we were asked to quote against other caterers but we always got the contract. Everything worked out, even better than we'd hoped, and we've gone from strength to strength.

It is fairly seasonal, of course. From March till the end of

October we're flat out. November is dodgy, January and February absolutely hopeless. So you've got to do a year's business in nine months, and you must build up a reputation to make sure you get what business is going. We land some very prestige bookings. Last year we organised a spectacular ball for hundreds of people and we were responsible for every detail, the marquee, tables and chairs, flowers, music, decoration, lighting and flood lighting as well as food and drink. Usually the only thing the client has to do is draw up a guest list and tell us what he wants. We can do the entire operation for him. We use sub-contractors who among them possess every skill and every piece of equipment that can possibly be required. The relationship between the client and myself becomes a very personal thing because I take over the whole responsibility. It's almost like being the host. We get to know each other very quickly and almost become friends for life. And when you've got that sort of relationship it means that people are very good about paying up. They don't keep me hanging about waiting because they know it's not just me who needs the money. I've got a lot of people depending on me to pay them. As well as the sub-contractors, I have a team of freelance helpers. There's Harriet who is the main cook, and Caroline, my sister, who is able to help me now that her baby is a little older. She's responsible for menu planning, cooking and shopping. And then there's Robert, an artist friend. He needs a part-time job to pay his rent and bills, so he works for me two days a week. He's in charge of wine stocks, and comes to all the parties to supervise the drinks. Besides this central group, I have a great crew of helpers. They're mostly young and attractive, wear pretty clothes and always look good. I don't go for the idea of little black dresses and white aprons. My helpers look like the guests. They all work so very hard that I make sure they have fun and enjoy themselves.

We've made a name for our good food and our sense of style, and consequently the bookings keep coming in. In the past eight months we've done 110 events. Tomorrow will be frantic, even busier than a typical day. At 9.45am eight of my staff will leave our Wiltshire headquarters and provide lunch for 141 members of the National Trust at Kingston Lacey, near Wimborne. Then they'll pack up, come home, unload, load up again with more food and drive to London. There's a charity dance and we're doing breakfast for a thousand people, quite a simple meal, orange juice, kedgeree, croissants and coffee. That will take them until about 3.30 in the morning. After that they'll all drive back to Wiltshire, and a team of five will set off to provide the President's Lunch, for sixty guests, at the Frome Show.

Most of our events are on a very large scale which means that we can run into cash flow problems. Normally we cater for an average of 180, and we would never charge less than £2.50 to £3.00 a head, usually more, so our bills are rarely less than £750, and since we have to buy the food in advance we can't afford to be kept waiting. Fortunately we've never had a bad debt. The biggest amount we ever earned for one function was £18,000 but for that I had to ask for £6,000 in advance so that I could get what I needed. I couldn't, wouldn't, have done it on any other terms. I only had to wait ten days for the other £12,000, so that worked out all right. The recession doesn't really seem to affect catering. Business organisations always need to spend money, and there are always private individuals who seem to want to spend, and have the money to spend. If they choose to spend it with me I'm not complaining! We do a big dinner for one of the sponsors of the Bath Festival every year. And we do the Wylye Horse Trials, which is another annual event. Wylye has become a great thing these days, very popular, and it attracts top riders, all the big names in the horse-riding world. It sounds fun but in fact we spend our time sitting in a tent on a very cold hill with minimal facilities. Every day, for five days, we provide lunch for 700 in the Members' Tent, and we lay on 'pub grub' for the public, approximately 400 of them. Besides that, we make breakfast for the competitors, and do an evening bistro for them every night – cheap, cheerful nosh for starving people who've spent the whole day on horseback in all sorts of weather. The menu's pretty basic and very cheap, stew and vegetables, plum duff, you know the sort of thing, but we run a bar too so there's always a party atmosphere.

Cowes has been our huge excitement this year. A friend of mine, who runs a very successful discotheque, was asked to lay on some sort of social activity for Cowes week. The facilities there used to be abysmal and they were always getting letters of

complaint because all these smart, well-heeled people who'd been
sailing all day had absolutely nothing to do and nowhere to go
when they were on shore. So we got together and decided to lay
on a sort of Wylye Horse Trials operation on Cowes Marina in a
tent. We had no idea what we were going to cater for but we
decided to do the lot – breakfast, lunch and dinner, and a bar
open all day. That meant a working day of eighteen hours. Ten
of us went to Cowes, stayed in a filthy pub and worked ourselves
into the ground. I was there for a fortnight. We more or less shut
up shop here except that two of the girls came back to do a
couple of bookings we were already committed to. We took a
refrigerated lorry with us, Calor gas ranges, all our equipment,
everything. It was the most tiring, hard-working function we've
ever done. To start with we tried to have an hour's rest each day,
from three till four o'clock in the afternoon, but we found that
just made us even more exhausted because we couldn't really
sleep, we just sat around feeling dead. In the end we decided the
best thing was to keep going for the full eighteen hours without a
break. You can do it if you know it's only going to be for a fortnight, but you couldn't keep it up for long. We just collapsed
afterwards. But it was a very lucrative engagement at what can be
a thin time of the year, and it worked. We've been asked to do it
again next August, and to lay on something special for the
Admiral's Cup, plus a Function Tent for sponsors and
promoters.

Catering is very hard work, especially the way we do it. The
pace is terrific, and you have to be young and fit. The hours are
anti-social and endless. I work seven days a week and up to
twenty-four hours a day. The only people I see are the people I
work with. There's never time for socialising, and I do miss my
friends. I took a weekend off a little while ago, but I got so
exhausted rushing around visiting all the friends I hadn't seen for
ages that at the end of it I was absolutely worn out and wished I'd
stayed quietly at home and got on with the job!

My main job is organisation and checking. I personally check
everything that goes out – again and again and again! I don't
think it's fair to put the blame on the cooks if anything goes
wrong. Once I've checked a dish I take the responsibility for it on
my shoulders. I can cook. Once, when we were pushed, I made

boeuf bourguignonne for 300 people. I reckon I could do about 75 per cent of the cooking if I had to, but running a business like mine is a huge organisational task. I've always been a fanatical organiser. Even at school I used to have a wall-chart day-planner so that I knew exactly when I should be doing my homework or starting to revise for exams. I've been the same all my life. I have check lists for everything. I must be methodical. Everything must be written down, and I guard my bookings diary with my life. But it pays off, you see, because fitting in every engagement, directing staff all over the country, planning ahead, sometimes a year ahead – as well as fitting in emergency bookings at about twenty-four hours' notice – all that needs someone who thrives on organisation. And I do thrive on it. I absolutely love it. It's fun – for the time being, at any rate, but not for ever.

Toni Chameau   Freelance Caterer

I've been interested in fine food and wine all my life. I suppose I enjoy cooking because I enjoy eating. I like being in a service industry, making people feel comfortable and happy.

When I was young my parents used to take me to the very best hotels and restaurants, the sort of places that were in the *Michelin Guide*, and I've always enjoyed the atmosphere of good hotels, the efficiency, care and luxury. After the war, my parents went into the restaurant business. My mother was an excellent cook, a really marvellous cook. I was involved in that and eventually my father said 'If you're really going to take this seriously you should get some proper training.' So I was sent off to a hotel school in Lausanne, and did a six-month course there, then went on to Lugano for practical experience. It was only eighteen months in all, not very long.

My parents moved on to run a really excellent pub which was listed in the *Good Food Guide*, and I helped them. Unfortunately they had to give up when my mother became ill, so I went off to Canada and worked in hotels. While I was there I met my husband, a Frenchman who was also in the hotel business. Eventually we came home and decided that we'd really like to run our own pub and build up a first rate restaurant. We had hardly any capital, so it wasn't easy, but eventually we managed to buy a place, in Birtle, Derbyshire, for £1,200. That was in 1958. The price was ridiculously low, of course, but there were good reasons for that. There was no mains water and no sewerage – the loos were buckets in the backyard! There was no car park, and the pub was situated at the end of a narrow, pot-holed lane. Anyway we took it on, and we made a go of it. Eventually we managed to acquire land for a big car park, and a water main was built through the village. We had the first mains water flush toilets and bath in the village. We were there for twenty years and built it up into a seventeen-bedroomed hotel with a first rate restaurant which had star rating in the *Michelin Guide*.

In 1978 I made a new start and came to Hampshire with my parents and my children. I was still fascinated by food, so I decided to teach part-time in the catering department of the local college of technology. I thought it would fit in with the demands of family life, but it wasn't for me. I was frustrated, and didn't enjoy it at all, not really, though the students were fun. However, in the meantime I had made friends with people who ran a local wine shop and did a bit of catering. They asked me to provide them with some food – pâtés and quiches – and I enjoyed that very much. When they decided to sell out, I bought the place from them in partnership with my son-in-law, and we went on doing both the retail selling of the delicatessen and the catering events. But the shop wasn't viable, not for the two of us to make a living from it. There just isn't enough luxury trade in a small country town. Our expenses went up and up, the cost of the premises, heating, rates, but we couldn't put up our prices accordingly because the customers just weren't prepared to pay for quality. What's more, they wouldn't get into the habit of ordering ahead, so we had to make small quantities in order to avoid wastage and then we'd find that we were out of what people decided they wanted on the spur of the moment, so we lost custom. The only way to make a profit, when you take in the labour factor, is to make large quantities. In a way, the customers destroyed the shop. People still quibble about costs. They have no idea how expensive first-rate food has to be. For instance, my speciality is quiche, made to order, and provided in a foil dish. I make a really good, rich quiche, using lots of eggs, cream, butter, a quarter of a pound of mushrooms, masses of top quality cheese, enough to serve six. Yet people complain if I charge £2. About 33½p per portion and they think I'm overdoing it – for *that* sort of quality.

Now I've closed the shop and I do all sorts of freelance catering – some freezer food to order, though the profit margin is low, wedding parties, cold buffets for up to 130, dinner parties for six to fourteen – that would be hot food – even barbecues. I enjoy them all, though I prefer the smaller events. For instance, a dinner party for six is enormous fun, though much less profitable than a big do. But money isn't my main interest. My children are off my hands now and I have a small unearned income, so I just need to make enough to top that up. What I value most is the social life it brings me, so I'm not as commercial as I ought to be. I get to know people I would never meet otherwise. I've made many personal friends. I'm nearly always treated as one of the guests. My clients ply me with food and wine. 'Do have a drink,' they say. 'Please have something to eat.' I have to resist, of course, otherwise I'd never be able to do the job properly, but they can't bear to think I'm having to work at their party. It's funny really.

That's the greatest satisfaction, the social contacts. Another is the fascinating projects that come my way. One of the things I love doing most is putting on super meals for tourists, often Americans visiting Salisbury on special English Heritage or Country Homes and Castles package holidays. Part of their tour includes meals in very special, beautiful, historic old houses, and it gives me a great thrill working in those lovely buildings and watching the delight with which the visitors absorb both the food and the atmosphere of their surroundings. Again, I meet some fascinating people, people I'd never normally come into contact with.

Another interesting job was providing the refreshments offered to potential customers and clients of a big national bank when they had a publicity stall at the New Forest show. Great fun! And I've just done my first barbecue and have another lined up soon. I did marinaded chicken legs, bacon, really good sausages, homemade beefburgers, garlic bread and a variety of salads. Then we finished off with fresh fruit salad and cream. I was anxious about the weather but they'd promised me some sort of shelter if it rained, so I said to myself, 'Well, girl, you'll just have to go in your wellies and make the most of it.' In the end I needn't have worried, the weather was perfect. The other problem was the amount of stuff I had to take – the food, china, cutlery, glass and my own barbecue. I thought I'd never get it all packed into my little estate car but I managed. I've decided that if business grows I'll buy a little trailer to attach to the back. I'm gradually building up all my own equipment, dishes, cutlery and so forth because it's so expensive to hire. If I have my own I can charge my customers less.

Fixing charges is a constant worry. I daren't price myself out of the market. If I'm doing a freezer order I simply double the cost of the ingredients. For a dinner party I charge double the cost of ingredients, plus £3 an hour for my time from the moment I leave home until I get back. But I do nearly all the preparation at home, of course, and as little as possible on the premises. For a wedding I fix the cost per head according to the menu they've chosen, plus the charge for my time, plus 3p for each item of my cutlery or crockery they use. That can be about 25p per head on top of the basic price. A finger buffet can be expensive because it's so fiddly and time-consuming to prepare – asparagus fingers and vol-au-vents, that sort of thing. It might be £3.50 a head, and sometimes people think that's too much to be charged by a small caterer like me, though a commercial caterer might quote double. The trouble is, when you're a freelance working from home they imagine you're an amateur, a housewife with an amusing hobby. In fact, I never let the customer come out worst when I'm doing my costing. If anyone's out of pocket it'll be me. I need their custom and their recommendation.

Personal recommendation is the best way of getting work if you can afford to wait for it. It takes time for people to get round to their next party, remember how you catered for the last celebration they went to, remind themselves of your name, get in touch with your mutual contact and then telephone or write to you. But it does mean that you're catering for the sort of market that interests you. The right sort of people recommend you to the right sort of people. I do advertise in our local papers but some of the replies need sifting very carefully. Many of the requests are absolutely impossible. I was once asked to put on a huge medieval banquet in a place which didn't even possess an oven. How I was supposed to transport those vast quantities of piping hot food, roast chicken and God knows what from my kitchen to their hired hall I don't know! I was also peeved that they wanted it to be genuine yet were proposing to include baked potatoes on the menu. Potatoes hadn't even reached this country in medieval times. I turned that booking down!

Besides the newspaper advertisements I have cards which I distribute like confetti, though I feel a bit shy about leaving them lying around in people's houses unless the hostess suggests it. I'm proposing to have book-matches printed for me very soon; they please me more because you're actually giving people something, a little gift which just happens to remind them of you! And I'm placing an advertisement in the Yellow Pages. This is expensive, but I've been told it can double your business so I hope it will be worth it.

You do need to be pretty well organised if you're to make a success of this sort of business. For instance, I take bookings about four months before the actual date. I go along and see the client and we discuss everything – what sort of meal they want, what they are prepared to pay, what specialities of my own they are interested in and how many guests they are expecting. The initial decision has to be whether they want a finger buffet, a fork buffet or a sit-down meal, and whether they are actually prepared to pay for what they want.

I start cooking about a week ahead. I don't like to use the deep freeze too much but for some things, it's essential. For instance, I can do pastry and quiche cases in advance and freeze them. I also order the food I need well ahead. I use the local shops as much as possible because I can trust them for quality. I'm able to examine the goods and they know I'll expect the best. I don't need to buy in vast quantities but even so, because I'm a good regular customer, people like the local butcher charge me hotel rates. Local business men also let me open accounts with them and this is useful. It helps me with my cash flow, and it's enormously useful for my accountant to have all my monthly invoices when he comes to do my books; it keeps everything in apple pie order. And the local shops are always ready to help out in an emergency; you're a person to them, not just a number. I do use the nearest Cash and Carry as well, but not a great deal.

When it comes to putting on the event I usually need a bit of help so I call on my family and friends quite often. My father is a splendid dishwasher! And I have a friend who is also a caterer and we give each other a lot of mutual support. If I'm pushed, she helps me. If she's overworked, I help her. But we always insist on paying each other, and putting the arrangement on a business-like basis.

Though the actual cooking and preparation of the food is very important, presentation is half the battle. If you please the eye, you please the palate. The guests begin to enjoy your food before they've tasted a forkful. Colour is very important. I decorate practically everything. Freshly chopped parsley and other herbs add colour and bring out the flavour. And I use slices of tomato and slivers of pepper. I even make a bed of forked-up aspic jelly with chopped parsley floating in it; it makes a lovely base, like a sea of green. I usually use large, high-quality foil dishes for serving the food on. They are patterned, and tough, but very light-weight, and come in several shapes and sizes. I get them in the Cash and Carry for between 60p and 90p each, but I can use them up to a dozen times if I'm careful and they really look good. I think china serving dishes have a lot of disadvantages. You can rarely get matching ones, and they are heavy, both for handling and for adding weight in the car which is usually down to the back axles anyway. And finally, they break. I'm not keen on doilies either; they just go soggy and get all mixed up with the bottom of the flan or cake and make them impossible to cut.

People do appreciate your taking pains to make their party look good, as I discovered quite recently. A lady came to see me and said that her husband wanted to celebrate their Silver Wedding with a special luncheon, at home, with their friends and family around them. The trouble was, he thought it would be fun but she thought it would be an awful lot of hard work. 'What I want you to do,' she said, 'is come in the morning, bring everything with you, and then afterwards take all that's left away with you. I want to enjoy the party too. I don't want to wash as much as a single glass.' Well, I did just that; I cleared up there, then brought all the dirty dishes back here and had a grand wash-up. Afterwards I got an absolutely charming letter from her, the most appreciative I've ever received. 'It not only tasted wonderful,' she wrote, 'it looked so good. All those wonderful colours and textures. A real picture!' I felt that was a little triumph. I can honestly say I haven't had many disasters. Only two spring to mind.

The first was when my son-in-law jammed a newly installed waste disposal unit, and the husband had to roll up his shirt sleeves, in the middle of his own party, and unblock it. The second was rather more serious. I had guests for a meal here and I served them some of my own liver pâté. It's very special, cooked ever so gently, then lightly whipped up with cream over a bowl of ice. My friend thought it delicious, and asked if she could buy some from my freezer. Of course I agreed and she took it away with her, absolutely delighted. Unfortunately she didn't go straight home. The next night she spent with other friends, and put the pâté in their fridge. The following night she spent with relatives and left the pâté on the mantelpiece in a warm room. A few days later we heard from the environmental health officer that she was suffering from salmonella poisoning and they thought my pâté was the source. And so it was, but it wasn't my fault. It should have been eaten as soon as it thawed, and she should have known that because she was a microbiologist. One has to be immensely careful about things like defrosting and not refreezing unfrozen things unless they've been cooked in the meantime. Food poisoning is a nightmare that is always lurking at the back of my mind because you never know what people, even the most sensible people, will do with food they've bought from your freezer. This is why I'm very well insured – a quarter of a million pounds' worth – for public liability. It's not a lot. I'd raise it to half a million if I could afford it. Just imagine, if you're sued for poisoning fifty people how far would quarter of a million go? It costs me £15 or £16 a year, and it's worth every penny. In fact, if I had to say which was the most important thing to consider in this business, that must be it – adequate insurance.

Jo Dickson 'Dickson and Donnelly'

I'm Australian, an occupational therapist by profession, but I married a farmer and settled in England. He really needs to have me at home helping him sometimes, and I like the freedom of being able to plan my own working hours and not to be tied to a regular routine. There's much more flexibility in freelance catering than in a 'proper job'. I had done a three months' Cordon Bleu course in London so I thought I might be able to cope with this sort of work.

I started about four years ago, beginning in a very small way with a girl friend, Christian. We called ourselves 'Country Catering'. At first we did mostly freezer cooking, but basically we discovered that, by the time we'd counted the hours of work we'd put in, the profits were minimal. You just can't charge too much; people don't think it's worth it. Freezer cooking can be very boring too because even if there are two of you it's usually easier to work in separate places, with two kitchens at your disposal and all your own equipment and machinery.

But there are advantages in beginning this way. You don't really need a lot of capital or equipment, so you don't have to worry about finding the money to get off the ground. Secondly, if you do a good job you get known and other work comes your way. We soon found that, through personal recommendation, we were being offered dinner parties and buffets. It was quite funny in the early days. We couldn't afford to employ people to help us so we used our husbands and families, dressed them up in dinner jackets or formal clothes and used them as butlers and waiters. They were very good. It was just like a game really, everyone laughed about it. We did bigger events too, including a party for the National Farmers' Union, I remember, for a hundred people. We had to hire all the equipment for that.

We did a little bit of advertising. We started with the local paper but the work we were offered through that wasn't what we wanted; it was very basic food, nothing exciting. Then we took a stand at the local agricultural show to advertise ourselves. We took menus and our deep freeze list, as well as lots of samples of our cooking. I know it sounds a good idea, but it wasn't. People just came along and ate up our food – lovely little profiteroles we'd slaved over, pâtés, all sorts of beautiful things – said how nice they were and then wandered off. We got absolutely no orders, so it was money down the drain really, except that we learned from the experience.

That first partnership dissolved when Christian had a baby, and I now have another partner, a man, and we've got everything worked out on a thoroughly professional basis. Really the business is growing amazingly well. I've stopped thinking of myself as an amateur. People do say you need three partners to avoid arguments but I find I get on very well in a twofold partnership. With Neil there are no arguments because our personal skills are very different. He's got expertise in areas where I haven't, and it's the other way round too, so we respect each other's judgement. He was catering manager for a big firm and then they installed food-vending machines so he became redundant. He knows all about organisation and large-scale planning, and with two of us we can take on a lot of work and divide our resources. He masterminds some of the events, I take charge of others.

The biggest booking we've had was for a wedding with three hundred guests, and soon we're going to provide refreshments for the club of our annual festival of the arts. That will run for a fortnight so it will be a lot of work, a real challenge. Again, the job came our way through personal contacts and recommendation. I don't think advertising brings in that sort of work. In fact, we don't need to advertise now, though we always leave cards.

We're just beginning to make money. We decided to build up a large stock of equipment instead of having to hire everything all the time, so for six months we ploughed all the profits back into the business. It's worth it in the long run. We still haven't got everything. Large tablecloths, for instance, are phenomenally expensive. We co-operate with other freelance caterers in the area. It's cheaper to hire from friends than from a commercial firm, and it's always a good idea to pool your resources with other people doing the same sort of thing rather than go in for cut-throat competition.

We try to think big because it's the big events that make the money. It may sound extraordinary, but it's possible to spend the same length of time, say twelve hours, preparing a dinner for twelve or a buffet for a hundred. It's the quality of work that puts up the labour costs. Anything fiddly and time-consuming can leave you out of pocket.

Presentation is vitally important. Everything must look good – snowy cloths, good napkins, flowers. You learn about this as you go, and it becomes second nature. No dish ever leaves the kitchen without some form of decoration or garnish, a little bit of greenery or colour.

It's not an easy job. It's very hard work, but, funnily enough, the hardest bit of all isn't the actual cooking, it's the physical slog of getting all the food and bits and pieces to the scene of the party, getting it organised and then getting everything home again. The worst part by far is clearing up at the end. The last engagement we had, I got home at 4.30am. My partner didn't get back till 6am. Sheer exhaustion! We do have a lot of extra hands, of course. We can call upon a team of twenty to thirty people to help. The two of us do all the cooking ourselves, but we pay people to come along and lend a hand with the setting out, serving and washing up. They nearly all have other jobs but enjoy working with us occasionally, wearing a different hat, as a sort of light relief. Most of them have had some experience of hotel work, perhaps holiday jobs in their student days, so they do quite well and have a lot of fun. One of them earns her living as ward sister in the intensive care unit of the infirmary, a different world. Another is a milkman. It was so funny, at a wedding lots of the guests recognised him as he refilled their glasses but most of them just couldn't place his face. Others did work out who he was, and you could just see them saying to each other 'What on earth is our milkman doing pouring our alcohol?' We all get on very well together. They are nearly all friends or friends of friends, people we know; we've never advertised for them. There's only ever been one problem. One girl quibbled about what we paid her. There was no unpleasantness, not really. We simply didn't use her again. We just can't afford to pay a large hourly rate, but most people understand that. They earn pocket money, they enjoy themselves and that's enough.

We insist on high standards in everything. We make sure our food looks as good as possible, and that our service is impeccable, friendly, courteous, efficient. We also use high-quality ingredients. For instance, all our vegetables are fresh. This is the sort of quality that customers are prepared to pay for in these days of convenience foods and freezer buying. Some of the made-up dishes that are always on our menus are cooked beforehand and kept in our freezers, of course. That's part of the way we organise ourselves. Good organisation is vital. It makes sense to cook ahead when you have time on your hands so that you're not caught on the hop when you run into a busy patch. Marketing is obviously very important too. The secret is to find a good supplier and to stick with him. We use one excellent greengrocer who we know we can rely on entirely. He has contacts all over the place, and if we give him a little advance notice he can get us practically anything we need, and always in tip-top condition. It's the same with the butcher. We usually receive our bookings about three months in advance, so as soon as the menu is decided we go and see him and tell him what we are going to need. He then keeps his eyes open while he's doing his marketing, and as soon as he sees the meat we want, the right price and the right quality, he gets it for us and it can stay in the deep freeze until it's needed. Apart from this, we rely quite heavily on our local Cash and Carry. It's less time-consuming than shopping around, and we usually notice when they've got a good bargain on their shelves.

We haven't had many problems so far. I think we've got our costings right. We work out the cost of our ingredients, double it and then add the cost of our labour at so much an hour. We have an accountant to advise us and keep our books straight. We have had occasional cash flow difficulties, but we managed to talk our bank manager into giving us overdraft facilities. At first he was very dubious. 'I've heard it all before,' he said. 'People like you, starting up in business, convinced you're going to make a profit. But how do I know you're a sound investment? Convince me.' So we produced our diary of future bookings, explained what we would charge, what our profit margin would be and projected earnings over the next six months or so – and he was convinced.

Fortunately, we have never had any trouble about being paid. We don't ask for a deposit, but the bill is normally settled within ten days. We are obviously very lucky with our customers. We carry very comprehensive insurance. That's terribly important.

Only the other day one of our helpers spilled wine on a lady's dress and we got an absolutely foul letter from her husband, berating us for clumsiness and saying he would send us the bill for cleaning. We don't have many disasters, though. I think the worst thing was during the terrible snow at the end of 1981. We had a party booked for a hundred people. At 3 o'clock on the day of the event the host telephoned and said he would have to cancel. The guests just couldn't get through because of the weather. All the food was ready by then, of course, and none of it could be frozen. Some of it we either ate ourselves or gave to friends, but a lot of it was wasted, and at that stage we had no insurance, no cover at all. That taught us a lesson. However, the outcome wasn't as bad as it might have been. Our customer paid the cost price of the actual food and rebooked the event for a later date.

All in all I get a lot of satisfaction out of the business. The main pleasure is getting it all together and seeing it work properly – the food, the general appearance, the timing, the mood. By the middle of the party you can tell whether it's a success. A lot of that success depends upon the attitude and deportment of myself, my partner and our staff, a group of friends, enjoying our work and giving enjoyment by it.

Joan Thompson 'Wooden Spoon'

We started nine years ago from very small beginnings. Now we're a pretty big organisation, very busy, a proper business. I have one partner, Judith, and we both have to work very hard. It began when I was working for a catering company which was providing directors' lunches for a local bank. I heard through the grapevine that the cricket club was looking for a caterer for their festival lunch, so I contacted the secretary and got the booking. Since then we've never looked back.

We didn't want a great deal of work to start with because we both had very young children and heavy family commitments. We didn't do any advertising at all but we were closely linked with Gloucester Cathedral (both our husbands are lay clerks there) and a lot of bookings came through them, for weddings, christenings, funerals and meals for societies like the Organists' Society. Now the link has become even stronger. Two years ago the dean and chapter asked us to run the refectory at the cathedral and we do that all week, Mondays to Saturdays, from 10.30am till 5pm. We do it on a rota basis with a part-time staff of ten, working not more than six or eight hours a week so that they don't exceed the taxfree limit.

The two businesses go hand in hand. The same people who staff the refectory are involved in the outside bookings, and we've now acquired a cook who works for us five mornings a week. A lot of the expenses are shared between the two concerns, and a lot of preparation for both organisations can be done at the same time. I don't think the refectory is as profitable as the outside catering, but it's very good advertising for us, a good shop window, and it brings in a lot of work. In fact, we don't need to do much advertising now, apart from our cards which we dish out liberally. When we began we advertised in our local evening daily paper under 'services'. Then we found that one job brought in another. But we've been placing an advertisement in the Yellow Pages for the last four years, and in that time we've doubled our turnover.

In the refectory we serve quite sophisticated food, everything homemade. We do lasagne, moussaka and chilli con carne, as well as quiches, toasted sandwiches, ploughman's lunches and a whole variety of salads, but no chips and no meat and two veg. That's not our style. We pay rent to the cathedral and have to pay back 10 per cent of their initial investment in the equipment and space we use.

The most difficult part of the job, I find, is organisation. Keeping everything going. Fortunately I did a three-year course in institutional management, and that's been invaluable. Judith and I have worked out a system in which we each have a week in charge. The one who's 'on' spends the morning in the refectory, supervising the staff, then in the afternoon there's the buying to do, and often cooking and paperwork in the evening. The one who's 'off' is under the control of the other, and more or less does what she's told, but she's not so busy. She'll still be involved in outside functions, making puddings, that sort of thing. The puddings are our speciality; mostly we use Cordon Bleu recipes, galette au chocolat, dacquoise with apricot sauce. The dean's wife's favourite is chocolate whisky gateau; we always make that for her. Our presentation is very simple, not all aspic, by any means. We don't do the flowers ourselves, but we have contacts with people who do. Our real satisfaction comes from the actual cooking – we both love it.

We share the paperwork, though we have an accountant, a solicitor, a proper partnership agreement and a helpful bank manager. Judith does the books and the VAT accounts. I do the 'quotes', there could be three a day. I present hand-written letters on smart, headed notepaper. The personal touch seems to be appreciated. And I send photocopied menus for people to choose from. We do finger buffets, cold fork buffets, hot fork buffets, table dinner service, cocktail savouries and freezer foods. The cheapest finger buffet would cost about £1.25 per head, plus VAT, and would consist of assorted sandwiches, sausage rolls, mushroom vol-au-vents, pizza fingers and crisps, nuts etc. The most expensive dinner could cost about £7.50. That might include scampi façon gourmet, filet de boeuf en croute with courgettes provençales and duchesse potatoes and butterscotch cream flan. Our freezer foods include some very special dishes – potage madrilene, iced cucumber, gazpacho, sauté beef in port, boîte au chocolat aux fruits, bombe Mexicaine and so on – recipes that people might not bother with themselves. The trouble with freezer foods is that they're not at all lucrative, but they make a useful extra, and there is a demand for them. And our cocktail savouries are exciting too – mushroom beignets, quichelettes, smoked salmon roulades.

People obviously like what we do because the bookings come rolling in, but there's enormous pressure. The weight of the business feels very heavy on our shoulders. One June weekend we had an incredible schedule, two weddings to cater for on the Saturday, two lunches on the Sunday, a very special tea for 200 on the Monday, when Princess Anne came to open the local museum, and then the Tuesday was Cathedral Friends' Day for which we had to prepare 140 suppers and 350 teas! And remember, we had to keep the refectory going all the time. The punchline came when a lady rang up on the Wednesday morning and said 'You haven't forgotten about my tea party this afternoon?

There'll be thirty of us.' 'Don't worry, it's all organised,' I lied in my teeth, having completely forgotten about it. But we got it arranged for her with no trouble at all. Tea for thirty was child's play after what we'd just been through.

It really needed tremendous organisation, that weekend. At the end of it we were absolutely shattered. Organisation is of supreme importance. We have to do a lot of liaising. We normally cook to order for the complete week's work ahead of us. Judith and I have a deep freeze each and these are a vital part of our equipment. If ever the staff have time on their hands they make sandwiches, which freeze very well. We can fit five hundred rounds of sandwiches into a freezer. Family holidays are always a bit of a problem. When they begin looming up we always have to work very hard in advance to make sure the one left holding the fort is well prepared and can cope.

So far we've been lucky and have avoided major catastrophes. Once we felt a bit uncomfortable about some salmon we served. It tasted fine but somehow didn't smell quite right. However, there were no complaints and no after effects. If there had been, thank heavens we were covered by insurance. Silly little things happen. Once Judith's young son put his hand right into the middle of a beautiful lemon mousse. Fortunately the shops were still open so we were able to buy a carton of cream and whip it up to fill the hole and make it look good. In fact, everyone took it for granted that it was supposed to look like that, and we were complimented on it.

The nicest thing about the work is that we enjoy it. We set ourselves very high standards, but naturally some jobs go better than others. We don't like doing sit-down meals, they're the most difficult. We don't go in for silver service and highly trained waitresses but, apart from that, we're game to try anything. The variety makes it worth while. Mostly we do buffets for up to two or three hundred people, but sometimes we'll do a dinner party for as few as six, cooking it from scratch in the customer's kitchen. Dinner parties don't make money, though, because we can't get the prices we ought to. We do our costing from experience and from basing our prices on what other people charge. You just can't command a high price where there's not a lot of money, and we certainly don't want to outprice ourselves. But

the money's not the most important thing, thank goodness, it's
the satisfaction, the fact that different challenges keep cropping
up. For instance, one of our most unusual jobs was organising
picnics for the reps who were manning stalls at our local Three
Counties Show. Now that was fun!

Jim Beauchamp   'Good Life'

We're comparatively new to this game and we're still experiment-
ing, I suppose, finding out what works, what pays, what we most
enjoy. Five years ago we lived in London. I was in computers.
Sally was a top-flight secretary. We were both very well paid,
successful, going places. We had no children, and no plans to
have any. We had bought ourselves a rather smart little house, in
a rather smart part of Town, had lots of friends and did a lot of
socialising.

I've always been a very keen cook. My mother taught me and
let me help her when I was home from school for the holidays,
and it has always been a joy for me, more of a game than work.
I've had no formal training at all but I devour cookery books.
They've always been my favourite reading, even at bedtime. And
I watch TV cooks. They leave me breathless with admiration, so
slick and assured. Sally's hopeless, she can hardly boil an egg, but
she's very good at organising things, getting things done. So we
did a lot of entertaining. It was our main hobby, and friends were
always raving about our dinner parties, queueing up to get
invited. We seemed to be having quite a good time. People were
quite envious of our life style. But then we realised there was
something wrong, a sort of disenchantment, I suppose – lots of
money, lots of fun, but absolutely no satisfaction. Not really. Not
deep down. I couldn't even garden, which was my second
passion, because all we had was a little courtyard, well, a
backyard to be brutally honest, though I managed to make it
quite pretty; 'chic', people called it!

Then one weekend we were driving in this area, through the
Malverns, and saw a 'For Sale' notice on this house with a huge
old walled garden and a bit of a field. We simply fell in love with
it. Love at first sight. It seemed like an impossible dream, living

in a place like this, but something made me remember the estate agent's telephone number. (I swear I didn't write it down, it just stuck.) I rang them up next morning and couldn't believe the price they were asking. It was ridiculously low, compared with London prices. Sally and I went out for supper that night, and started talking. We went home to bed, and continued talking. Talked all night. By the time I was up cooking bacon and eggs, and brewing up very strong coffee, we'd decided we could do it. We had no commitments, nobody to be responsible to except ourselves. We knew we could sell our own house for a ludicrously inflated price and buy this place outright – no mortgage. First headache over. We'd have enough land to grow a lot of our own food, maybe even keep hens, and have bees. Bliss! And since it was in a very lovely area we could take paying guests during the season and turn it into a sort of guest house.

Everything went more or less according to plan, but we hadn't got it right. The paying guests rolled up all right; we had to turn them away in droves. But I fed them so well that we hardly made any profit. We weren't really charging Cordon Bleu prices but they were scoffing Cordon Bleu food. But that wasn't what really got me, because money wasn't the main thing. No, what infuriated me was that I'd make something really wonderful – a beautiful, delicate, salmon mousse, say – and they'd have the gall to ask for the tomato ketchup! Tomato ketchup, can you imagine? I used to get so furious Sally was scared I'd be charged with 'grievous bodily' with a sauce bottle before the season was over!

Some of them were appreciative, of course, and word must have got round that the food was pretty good, because one day I was down at the local and a bloke said 'Look, we don't want to stay at your place because we live here, but we would like to come in for a meal. Do you allow non-residents into your dining room?' Well, we didn't, but we thought, why not? Let's have a go. So we tried that for a while. But that wasn't quite right either. We began to feel that our house was being completely overrun by strangers, and it was difficult to fit in everybody and time the meals right. The strains and stresses and irritations began to get even worse than London, which was just ridiculous. I wasn't even finding time to garden properly, and we had planned to have all our own fresh vegetables and fruit. (The hens and bees have never materialised, not to this day, though we still live in hope.)

Then, after about a year, we re-thought the whole thing. Sally had this brilliant idea. Why not have paying guests who were really interested in food, either professionally or on an amateur basis, and do 'cooking holidays', show them how it's done, and then we could charge extra for tuition? And I had this brilliant idea – why not provide dinner for people in their own homes instead of our own, then we wouldn't have them cluttering up the place all the time? And that's more or less how it's working out now, and it's working well. So well that we are flooded with bookings, and absolutely refuse to accept them all because we keep in sight, every day, that we are doing this for our own pleasure, that money's not our first aim, that we must have time to enjoy life and be ourselves, and sometimes be by ourselves.

Our speciality is superb dinner parties, for up to twenty people, no more. We charge £10, £15 or £20 a head, depending upon the number of courses we provide, the choice of menu we give, the complexity of the dishes and whether we provide cutlery, crockery, napery, flowers etc. We sometimes even take tapes along, and play wonderful classical music while the guests eat. That's fun, choosing the music to match the food. For some people that's our particular hallmark. Makes us different from the run of the mill, I suppose.

An expensive meal might start with chilled cucumber soup, followed by grilled trout, then lemon sorbet as a remove, a boeuf bourguignonne or daube perhaps, a sweet trolley with several gateaux, bombes and ice puddings, fresh fruit, and a really varied cheeseboard, top-quality cheeses from both this country and abroad. Then, coffee and handmade mint chocolates to finish. And all the fruit and vegetables would be from our own garden. We have two huge freezers and everything we grow is used, including a huge variety of unusual herbs. *The Penguin Freezer Cookbook* is our Bible, so a glut of lettuce turns into lettuce soup; cucumbers might be baked or made into a ragout; strawberries, which tend to turn mushy when they thaw, are frozen as mousses or purées for ice-creams, sauces and sorbets.

The cookery school goes hand in hand with all this because the students actually help us to prepare the dinner parties. You might think this sounds like cheap labour and I used to feel pretty guilty about it, but the truth is, they want to do it and beg to be involved. They learn much more, you see, from actually doing the job under real conditions than learning about it in the clinical surroundings of a perfect kitchen where there's no pressure of time, no urgent need to cope with disasters. In fact, I think a lot of them find a dinner party the high spot of the whole week or fortnight they spend with us, and feel cheated if we haven't got a booking. They like to come along and waitress and butle and get really stuck in, and they feel cock-a-hoop when it goes well. One night an American girl said to me as I was driving them home (we've got a dormobile that we cram with food and people) 'Gee, that was great. Exciting as having a baby, I guess!' Not that I'd know!

The students even help in the garden, though that's not really supposed to be part of the course. But they love exploring the range of stuff we grow, the less common vegetables, mangetout peas, French beans, courgettes, asparagus, artichokes, and all the herbs, as well as strawberries, raspberries, masses of currants, gooseberries, plums, apples, pears – you name it, we probably grow it.

Things work well with Sally and me too. In the kitchen, I'm chief cook, she's bottle washer, strictly the menial, the dog's body. But in the office, she's the boss and I lick the stamps. She's formidably efficient, and has got the whole thing taped, running like clockwork. She scares the pants off me when she's on the warpath. We have very different skills. We're proud of our own and we respect each other's – a perfect partnership. And I'll tell you something, I wouldn't swop my Kenwood Chef for a computer now, not for all the tea in China.

Recommended Reading

Atterbury, Stella. *Leave it to Cook* (Penguin, 1968)
Bowen, Carol. *The Giant Sandwich Book* (Hamlyn, 1981)
Broughton, Kathleen. *Pressure Cooking Day by Day* (Pan, 1977)
Cadwallader, Sharon and Ohr, Judi. *Whole Earth Cookbook* (Penguin, 1972)
Elliot, Rose. *Not Just a Load of Old Lentils* (Fontana, 1976)
Ellis, Audrey. *Table Layout and Decoration* (Ward Lock, 1978)
Fawcett, Hilary. *The Good Food Guide's Dinner Party Books* (Consumers' Association, 1979)
Golzen, Godfrey. *Working for Yourself* (Kogan Page, 1980)
Hughes, Joyce and Eyton, Audrey. *The Low Calorie Menu Book* (Slimming Magazine, 1980)
Leith, Prue and Waldegrave, Caroline. *Complete Cookery Course*, 3 vols (Fontana, 1980)
Marks, James F. *Barbecues* (Penguin, 1977)
Nilson, Bee. *Making Ice-cream and Cold Sweets* (Mayflower, Granada, 1976)
Norwak, Mary. *The Complete Book of Barbecues* (Futura, 1975)
– *Deep Freezing Menus and Recipes* (Sphere, 1970)
Norwak, Mary and Mossman, Keith. *Growing, Freezing and Cooking* (Sphere, 1976)
Prince, Jean. *The Colour Book of Party Cooking* (Octopus, 1980)
Roden, Claudia. *Picnic: The Complete Guide to Outdoor Food* (Penguin, 1981)
Rose, Evelyn. *The Entertaining Cookbook* (Fontana, 1980)
Rubinstein, Helge and Bush, Sheila. *The Penguin Freezer Cookbook* (Penguin, 1973)
Spry, Constance and Hume, Rosemary. *The Constance Spry Cookery Book* (Dent, 1978)
Thomas, David St John. *The Breakfast Book* (David & Charles, 1980)
Wallace, Evelyn. *Cake Decorating and Sugarcraft* (Hamlyn, 1975)
Weatherall, J. and Marchetti, E. *The Lunchbox Book* (Circle Books, 1981)

Index